T0128819

Song of the Silent Bell

Song of the Silent Bell

*My parents' memoirs: Their separate roads
to survival during the Holocaust era*

Judy Cohen

SONG OF THE SILENT BELL
MY PARENTS' MEMOIRS: THEIR SEPARATE ROADS
TO SURVIVAL DURING THE HOLOCAUST ERA

iUniverse books may be ordered through booksellers or by contacting:

iUniverse
1663 Liberty Drive
Bloomington, IN 47403
www.iuniverse.com
1-800-Authors (1-800-288-4677)

Because of the dynamic nature of the Internet, any web addresses or links contained in this book may have changed since publication and may no longer be valid. The views expressed in this work are solely those of the author and do not necessarily reflect the views of the publisher, and the publisher hereby disclaims any responsibility for them.

ISBN: 978-1-4917-9305-3 (sc)
ISBN: 978-1-4917-9310-7 (e)

Print information available on the last page.

iUniverse rev. date: 07/27/2016

Dedicated to the six million Jews murdered in the Holocaust during World War II

Contents

Dedication

I want to dedicate this book to my mother, Olga Kay, a selfless and compassionate woman who has spent her life, first and foremost, looking out for other people before herself. Her only concern has always been to do for others, despite the pain and suffering she endured during her life. When my father's health began to decline, my mother was always at his side. There was no one that took better care of him. Her desire to help others and the values she imbued in my sister and me has always been an inspiration to me. I want to say thank you for being you.

Acknowledgments

I would like to thank the following people for their help.

Juli Elroie Kristof – for her wonderful translations of the poems and manuscripts, helping to shed light on the hidden documents.

Olga Kay – my mother, for taking over so I could spend more time on the book.

Evelyn Hefetz – my sister, who always came through for me when I couldn't find the right words.

Avi Haupt – for giving me the initial encouragement to write this book.

Gila Green and Ruth S. Almog – for helping me organize, refine, and finally prepare my manuscript for publication.

Pearl Goldberg – for tirelessly preparing the family trees, a task I couldn't have managed myself.

Dovev Hefetz – a talented artist, for designing the cover of the book.

Song of the Silent Bell

By Judy Cohen

Your life has come and gone
Taken by a passing breeze
Carrying with it
The touch of a gentle kiss

As the book opens
The sparks of poetic glitter escape their captivity
Reaching soaring heights
And meet where the musical chimes converge

Images emerge from a whirlpool of turmoil
Exploding and shattering into a thousand different lights
As the song of the silent bell rings out

The angry lion pounces in anger
And then drops in its eternal shame
The bitter seeds, long buried under the sand come to light
Cushioning the thorny pathway of G-d's tapestry

The call of the timeless wanderers
Echoes the agony of the tear-drenched ashes
You journeyed across eight stepping stones
Leading into the mist
And disappeared from us forever

My Father's Secret Book of Poetry

"Grandma, Grandma!" My seven-year-old grandson Itai ran into the kitchen. He couldn't wait to share the good news with me. "I beat Papa at chess again!" I looked at my father and saw the twinkle in his eye. He could no longer move his incapacitated body but his eyes were dancing with happiness.

On December 1, 2013, my father, George Kay, passed away peacefully at my house in Sha'arei Tikva, Israel, two days before his 94th birthday. A few months later, I went with my mother, Olga, to help clean out their apartment in Netanya, a city located in the northern central region of Israel. As we were sorting through my father's papers, we discovered an old, tattered notebook filled with his hand-written, native Hungarian. My mother, also a native of Hungary, began reading through the journal curiously. After some time, she looked up at me in awe. Puzzled by her expression, I asked my mother what she had read.

"It looks like poetry and letters", she answered. Her eyes looked at me questioningly as she ran her hands through her hair, obviously perplexed. "I had no idea he was so gifted. He never told me about this. Never mentioned that he wrote poetry."

I carefully took his notebook and gazed at it searchingly. Its cover was cracked and the pages inside yellowed with age. Since I could not read Hungarian, all I could do was stare blankly at my father's handwriting. Some entries were written in blue or black ink. Others in pencil. I was trying to imagine my father - such a quiet man - having a secret gift from G-d which he had never shared with anyone. Not even his wife. I asked my mother if she could translate some of it. She tried but it was too difficult for her since English is not her mother tongue.

We continued sifting through the rest of the papers for other written works but did not find anything.

The first thing I wanted to do was translate his poetry into English. My mother was thrilled with the idea. After making a few inquiries, I hired a lovely, young native Hungarian woman named Juli Elroie Kristof and sent her a copy of my father's thirty page manuscript.

Two long months after my mother and I had first discovered his writings, after waiting impatiently to read his work, Juli finally sent us the completed translation of my father's journal. As I read my father's poetry in English, I was struck by the power and emotion that exuded from his words; both characteristics so contrary to the person we thought we had known. The thought of leaving my father's poetry lying in a drawer seemed so unjust, but maintaining the secrecy of his hidden talent fit exactly who he was. He would never have wanted any praise. However, despite his having chosen to keep his writings private, I have chosen to publish them, albeit quietly and modestly.

The poems and letters in his notebook were dated from 1940 to 1946. Those were the years my father had spent in Palestine. We didn't find any other of his works written before or after those years. I still often wonder why he wrote only during this period. Perhaps it was the turmoil he had experienced during those years that brought out the poet in him. The passion he put into his writing touched me profoundly. Having my own affinity for poetry, I felt like I understood the intense need he had for writing at that time in his life. I lamented not being privy to this part of my father's personality while he was alive and I felt that writing this book would help me grieve. My sister, Evelyn, and I both have children and grandchildren who knew my father. It is important for me to document his works so that his grandchildren and great-grandchildren can learn about the side of him they never knew.

As I pondered over the idea of publishing my father's works I thought of my mother's own compelling story of survival, the story my sister and I had been hearing since we were children. I knew then that I needed to put both stories down in writing. This book contains the memoirs of my mother, and my father, and the tragic fates of their families. My mother is a Holocaust survivor, who endured the horrors of three concentration camps. My father escaped Hungary on the *Sakarya*, one of the largest ships that brought illegal Jewish immigrants to Palestine at the beginning of 1940.

I decided to write my parents' memoirs not only to help preserve the Holocaust memories of a generation that is dying out, but also to incorporate my father's literature and breathe new life into the poetry that had been lying locked away and dormant for almost sixty years. The chimes of his bell will be silent no more.

Judy Cohen

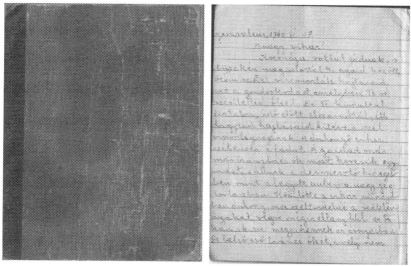

The cover of my father's notebook and a page from it.

About this Book

In addition to finding my father's journal, my mother and I found many of his old documents, well preserved and carefully put away, such as his Hungarian passport with the forged visa that allowed him to leave Europe, travel documents he needed to get to America, telegrams, and newspaper articles. That was my father; always very organized. Looking back, it seems to me now that he intentionally and perhaps ironically, prepared everything I needed for this book.

Pre-war photos from my mother's family are photographs my grandfather sent to his siblings, then residing in the Unites States. My mother's sister, Bella, was miraculously able to hide some photos of her young son (murdered in Auschwitz) while she was incarcerated in the Bergen-Belsen concentration camp.

Pre-war photographs from my father's side are photos my father, his brother, Laci, and his sister, Bözsi, took with them when they left Europe at the beginning of 1940. In addition, my father's cousin, Shlomo Haupt, succeeded in preserving his treasured family album while he was in forced labor camps.

My mother's Holocaust testimony, as documented in this book, was videotaped by the Survivors of the Shoah Visual History Foundation, established by Steven Spielberg, and integrated into Yad Vashem's film and testimony collection.

In July, 2004, when my father was eighty-five, my sister, Evelyn, interviewed him about his childhood in Hungary and his journey to Palestine on the *Sakarya*. My father was a man of few words and provided only limited information. The little information I have about him is taken from this interview, his book of poetry that we found, and the documents he preserved.

This book includes testimony of my father's niece, Malka (Bözsi's daughter), who was on the *Sakarya* with him. She was seven years old at the time and had documented her testimony several years before she died in 2011.

My father's testimony did not include any information about how the *Sakarya* was organized. Those details were taken from historical sources. The sections of this book describing the escape to Palestine on the *Sakarya*, combine historical facts, with first-hand testimonies of my father and Malka.

What this book does not have is the testimony of most of the Holocaust survivors from both my mother's and father's families. Except for my mother, my mother's sister, Adele, and my father's cousin, Shlomo Haupt, no one spoke about their experiences in the camps. This was a very common reaction among Holocaust survivors. Many felt ashamed or guilty of surviving while their families were murdered. For some, the atrocities they witnessed were just too painful to remember. For others, talking about it revived agonizing memories of their dead relatives. The subject for most Holocaust survivors was off limits.

Prologue

Growing up as a teenager in the 1930's in Nazi-occupied Europe, my father's life was thrown into chaos and loneliness. At the beginning of 1940, when he was 20, he was given the opportunity to escape Hitler's ovens. He chose to save himself and flee Europe, knowing that remaining meant almost certain death.

The guilt he felt about leaving his father, his sister, and the rest of his extended family to their fates at the hands of the Nazis, haunted him for the rest of his life to the point where he questioned whether he even had a Jewish soul or heart. His mother had died five years earlier, his father felt that he was already too old to start his life in a different country, and his sister Aranka's husband did not want to leave his parents behind. My father's brother, Laci, had gone to America just before my father left Hungary. In his poetry, he unforgivingly refers to himself as a coward and relentlessly blames himself for letting the fear for his own life lead him to abandon not only his family, but also his fellow European Jews.

In 1940, he escaped war-ravaged Europe on the *Sakarya*, together with another 2,300 Jewish refugees, and reached Palestine. He felt lost in his new surroundings and could not find himself after being torn from his family and uprooted from his native country. He took to writing poetry as a way of coping with the torment and emptiness that had engulfed his life, and to articulate his yearning for his family in Hungary.

In his writings, my father describes the turmoil in the world, his longing for peace, and in painful honesty, his most intimate inner struggles. He used his poetry to shout out to the world, in his own silent way.

After Evelyn read the translation of our father's poetry, she said to me, "It is fascinating, yet surreal. I still can't believe he wrote all this.

Just the style of the writing and all the metaphors is so unlike the person we knew. What interesting thoughts and ideas. I only remember him voicing his views on politics. He also sounded lost in many ways; where he was, what was going on around him, and he was so lonely. The poem he wrote about his mother expresses how passionately he still missed her and the rest of his family."

While we were growing up in the United States, my father rarely spoke about himself. He was emotional but very quiet. He did not verbally express his feelings. He kept everything locked up inside.

After spending six years in Palestine, he left for New York to be near his brother, Laci. In his interview, my father mentions that not long after arriving in New York, he realized that he did not want to remain there forever. He said that he had missed the Jewish way of life in Palestine and vowed one day to return. Unfortunately, the interview was not more specific. I think he missed living in all-Jewish towns and cities and took pride in watching Jews, for the first time, being given the chance to protect themselves. He also may have missed speaking Hebrew. After I moved to Israel at the age of nineteen, I remember him commenting how proud he was to hear me speaking Hebrew.

Thirty-nine years later, after rebuilding his life in New York, he eventually found his way back to Israel.

Chapter 1

My Father's Story

Each Person is an Entire World

The murder of six million Jews is impossible to fathom. Judaism teaches us that each person is an entire world. During the Holocaust, millions of worlds were destroyed. I included the family trees and the family histories of both my parents, to give a name, and where possible, a face, to a handful of those six million people.

"All passes without a trace. The storm sweeps everything away but the song remains the same forever."

My father in Palestine, 24 years old.

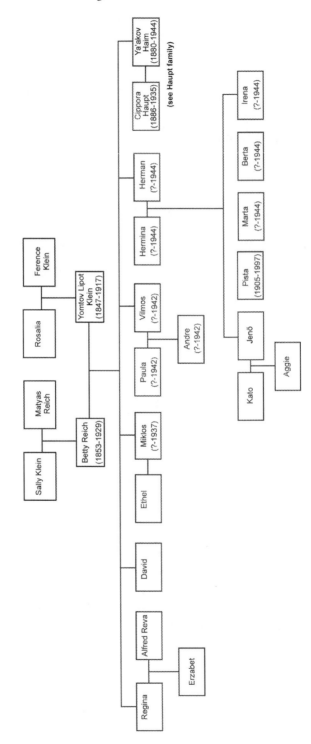

Klein Family

THE KLEIN FAMILY

My father, George Kay, was the son of Ya'akov Haim Klein and Cippora Haupt. Ya'akov Klein, was the son of Betty Reich and Yom Tov Lipot Klein. Yom Tov Lipot Klein, 1847-1917, was the son of Ference and Rosalia Klein. Betty Reich, 1853-1929, was the daughter of Matyas Reich and Sally Klein.

Betty and Yom Tov had six children, one daughter and five sons:

Regina married Alfred Reva. They had a daughter named Erzabet. Their fate is unknown.

David died of leukemia when he was very young.

Miklos married Ethel. He died of leukemia, in 1937.

Vilmos married Paula and had a son named Andre. They lived in, Czechoslovakia and were deported to Auschwitz in 1942, where they perished.

Herman married Hermina and moved to Balassagyarmat. They had five children:

Three daughters: **Marta**, **Berta**, and **Irena**. The three daughters and their parents Herman and Hermina, all perished in the Holocaust.

Two sons:

Jenő survived the Holocaust and married Kato after the war. They moved to Sweden and had a daughter named Aggie.

Pista (1905 – 1997) survived the war and remained in Hungary. He was very well-known by the Jews because he took care of the cemetery in Balassagyarmat and also helped build a museum in memory of the Jews that perished in Balassagyarmat.

Ya'akov Haim – my father's father (September 16, 1880-1944) perished in Auschwitz. He was married to Cippora Haupt and had four children, Bözsi (1908 – 1966), Laci (1909 – 1996), Aranka (1912 – 2007), and my father, George (1919 – 2013).

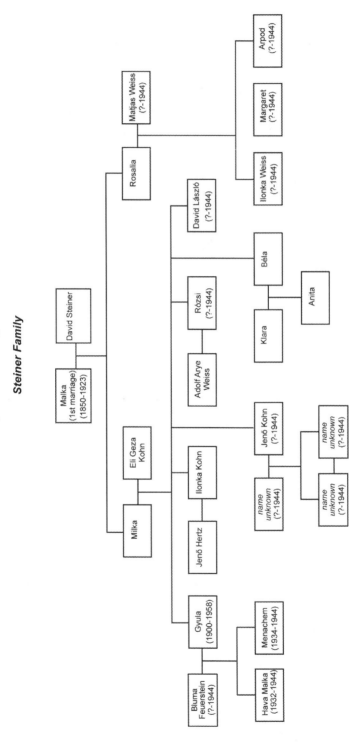

Malka Haupt's first marriage to David Steiner

Steiner Family

THE STEINER FAMILY – MALKA HAUPT'S FIRST MARRIAGE

My father's mother, Cippora Haupt, was the daughter of Binyamin Ze'ev Haupt (1842 – 1935) and Malka Yonas (1850 – 1923). Binyamin Ze'ev was Malka's second husband.

Malka's first husband was David Steiner, and they had two children, **Milka** and **Rosalia**.

Milka Steiner married Eli Geza Kohn. Milka is buried in Salgótarján.

What is known about Milka's husband Geza is that he became very ill and was hospitalized in a Catholic hospital in Pásztó. At that time, Cippora Haupt's brother, Nachman Zvi Haupt, his wife, Perla, and their two children, Shlomo and Ibi (Malka), were living in Pásztó. When Geza felt he was going to die, he sent a postcard and asked the Haupts if he could come to stay with them. They welcomed him to their house. He died in the Haupt home and is buried in Pásztó.

Milka and Eli Kohn had six children:

Gyula married Bluma Feuerstein and they had two children, Hava Malka and Menachem. His wife and children were deported and perished in Auschwitz. Only Gyula survived the war.

Ilonka Kohn married Jenő Hertz and they both escaped to Sweden in 1938.

Jenő Kohn (Milka's son) was married and had two children. The entire family died in Auschwitz.

Rózsi married Adolf Arye Weiss and lived in Cserhátszentiván. Adolf survived the war but his wife Rózsi perished in Auschwitz.

Béla survived the war and married Klara. They moved to Sweden and had a daughter named Anita.

David László was killed during the war while trying to cross the border into Sweden.

Rosalia married Matjas Weiss and they had three children: **Ilonka**, **Margaret**, and **Arpod**. Rosalia is buried in Hatvan, Hungary and the rest of the family perished in Auschwitz.

Milka Steiner Kohn

Eli Geza Kohn

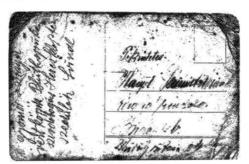

In the postcard which he addresses to Mr. Haupt, he writes that he is spitting up blood, has heart palpitations, and stomach aches, and he is dizzy.

Gyula Kohn and Bluma Feuerstein Kohn

Gyula and Bluma's children, Hava Malka and Menahem

Milka's son, Béla, stands next to Cippora
Haupt Klein's grave, Hungary, 1968.

Malka Haupt's second marriage

to Binyamin Ze'ev Haupt

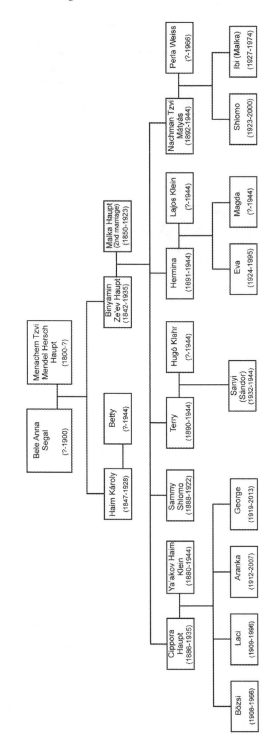

MALKA HAUPT'S SECOND MARRIAGE

Malka Haupt's second husband was Binyamin Ze'ev Haupt. Binyamin Ze'ev was born to Menachem Tzvi Mendel Hersch Haupt and Bele Anna Segal. They lived in the town of Cserhátszentiván, Hungary. Bele Anna died in 1900 and is buried in the Jewish cemetery in Cserhátszentiván.

Bele Anna and Menachem Tzvi Haupt had another child named Haim Károly. Haim married Betty and had one son. Betty, Haim's wife, perished in the Holocaust in 1944. Haim is buried next to his mother in the Jewish cemetery in Cserhátszentiván.

Malka and Binyamin Ze'ev Haupt had five children:

Cippora Haupt (1886-1935), my father's mother, was the eldest child. She died of cancer in 1935. She was born in Cserhátszentiván and was married to Ya'akov Haim Klein.

Sammy Shlomo (1888-1922) died of tuberculosis which he contracted as a soldier in the Hungarian army during World War I.

Terry (1890 – 1944) married Hugó Klahr and they had a son named Sanyi (Sándor). All three perished in Auschwitz.

Hermina (1891 – 1944) married Lajos Klein. They had two daughters, Eva and Magda. Only Eva survived the war.

Nachman Tzvi Mátyás (1892-1944) married Perla Weiss. They had two children, Shlomo and Ibi (Malka). Nachman Tzvi perished in the war but his wife and two children survived.

Cippora Haupt, 14 years old.

Terry and Hugó Klahr in front
of their grocery store.

Wedding of Nachman Tzvi Haupt and Perla Weiss, 1922
Front row (l-r): Bözsi (daughter of Cippora Haupt), Gyula Kohn, unknown female,
unknown male with little girl, the bride Perla Weiss, the groom Nachman Zvi Haupt,
Malka Haupt and her husband Binyamin Ze'ev Haupt, Milka Steiner Kohn, Cippora
Haupt Klein, Laci, (the young boy standing at the right, Cippora's son)

My Father's Childhood in Hungary

My father, George Kay, was born George (György) Michael Klein in Szécsény, Hungary, in 1919. Szécsény is a small town about seventy-five kilometers from Budapest. At the time my father lived there, it had a population of somewhere between 4,000 - 6,000 people, among them, 382 Jews.

He was the youngest of four children. His parents, Ya'akov Haim Klein and Cippora (Haupt) Klein, settled in a small house next to a railway station where they had a bar and a restaurant. In the interview he gave my sister, my father said, "As far as I remember, I spent most of my childhood, until the age of 19, in the restaurant my parents owned, where we also lived. Everyone in the family helped out with running the restaurant."

My father's family in front of their restaurant, 1930.
Back row (l-r): My father's mother Cippora, his brother Laci, his father Ya'akov Haim.
Front row (l-r): My father's sister Bözsi, my father, his sister Aranka.

The railroad tracks at the Scécsény train station; my father's house is at the right.

His family managed to get a permit from the Hungarian Train Association to open the bar and restaurant. Their many patrons were mainly transient passengers passing through town on trains that were constantly coming in and out of the station from Budapest and other places. They served both food and alcoholic drinks. Under Hungarian law at the time, it was mandatory for bars to be open seven days a week, twenty-four hours a day. My father came from a religious family and they observed *Shabbat*[1] as much as they could. They kept a kosher kitchen, but served non-kosher products as well. This was kept separately in the *kocsma* (bar) section of the restaurant where they served the customers. On *Shabbat* and Jewish holidays, when observant Jews are supposed to refrain from working, my grandparents hired a gentile worker to run the restaurant. I imagine they took turns for nightshifts, or they may have done all the cooking beforehand so that whoever took the night shift merely had to serve.

My father and all his siblings received different levels of education. After elementary school, Bözsi, Aranka, and my father continued studying in polgári (junior high school). Laci went on to study at gimnázium (high school).

When my father finished polgári, he went to Salgótarján, a larger city about thirty kilometers away, to study to be a dental technician with a man named Mr. Löwinger. His sister, Bözsi, got married in 1932 to Erno Bretter and they went to live in Salgótarján. Their first child, Malka, was born in 1933. During the week my father lived with his sister Bözsi, and her family. On Friday evenings and Saturday afternoons, he would eat the *Shabbat* meals with his mother's sister, Aunt Hermina, and her family, who also lived in Salgótarján. On Sundays he rode his bicycle to Szécsény to help his parents at the restaurant. Riding that road home was arduous because the road was mainly uphill and half of the time he had to carry his bicycle.

He studied in Salgótarján for approximately three years. In 1937, he went to work in Budapest where he was a metal caster for almost two years. There, he lived with his cousins, the Braun family.

In the early 1930s my father's brother, Laci, decided to study medicine. Then, universities in Hungary had quotas severely limiting the number of Jewish students and Laci was unable to gain admission to medical school there, so he went to study medicine in the cities of Padua and Bologna in Italy. He spent his last years of study in Rome where he received his medical degree.

During the weekends when my father was at home, he used to love going to *shul*[2] with his mother. "My mother lit candles every Friday night and we went to *shul* every week on Shabbat. I also remember

---

[1] The Hebrew word for the Jewish Sabbath.
[2] Synagogue

going to *Slichot*[3] with my mother. *Slichot* is usually recited between midnight and dawn so we would get up to go to *shul* at four o'clock in the morning when it was still very dark. Our *shul* was very beautiful. My sister, Aranka, got married in that *shul* in 1937 to her first husband, Laci Feuerstein. Unfortunately, it was destroyed under Hitler."

My father's sister Aranka, with her first husband, Laci Feuerstein.

My father, 13 years old, in his school uniform.

Demolished synagogue in Szécsény, destroyed in 1944[4].

---

[3] Penitential prayers that are recited before dawn during the week preceding Rosh Hashanah, the Jewish New Year.

[4] Reprinted with permission from A magyarországi holokauszt földrajzi enciklopédiája. Randolph L. Braham, ed. (Budapest: Park Könyvkiadó, 2007), p. 779.

Cippora Haupt Klein, My Grandmother

My father spoke very little about his mother. I rarely heard him express his feelings for her. How I wish now that I had asked him questions while he was still alive. It pains me to know that I have lost the opportunity to learn about her. I've always missed not having grandparents! They are the empty part of my life that can never be filled.

Only through his poetry does my father reveal how devastated he was by his mother's death. After reading the heart-wrenching poem he wrote about her, I could understand the depths to which he loved her. Unfortunately, my grandmother suffered from cancer and died very young in 1935 at the age of forty-nine. She was buried in Szécsény.

In 1935, Bözsi's daughter, Malka, was two-and-a-half years old. Years later, she remarkably recalls her first memory: "The first memory I have is the day my grandmother Cippora died. She was forty-nine years old. She was lying on a big bed and a lot of people were standing around her, crying. I was sitting on a small bench in front of the bed."

Klein family, 1934. Back (l-r): Laci, my grandmother Cippora, Bözsi's daughter Malka, my grandfather Ya'akov Haim, my father. Front (l-r): Bözsi, Aranka.

Cippora Haupt Klein.

The Rise of Anti-Semitism in Hungary

In 1938, the Hungarian government began passing anti-Jewish legislation restricting the number of Jews who could be employed and gradually revoking all business licenses. While my father worked in Budapest during the years 1937-1938, he witnessed the rise of anti-Semitism. "Many right-wing Hungarian organizations demonstrated against the Jews and broke windows of Jewish businesses. I also saw Jewish men and women being abused on the streets by Hungarian soldiers."

"It affected our family business as well. At the beginning of 1938, a train load of soldiers pulled into the station, entered our restaurant, and started to ransack the place. My sister, Bözsi, was in the restaurant with her daughter, Malka. While the soldiers were wreaking havoc, it was impossible for Bözsi to leave the restaurant so Malka, who was only five years old at that time, went to look for some policemen in the hope that they would stop the rampage. Malka finally found two policemen and asked them to come and stop the soldiers, but they only laughed (at the thought of coming to the aid of a Jew)! Afterwards, the soldiers finally left the restaurant and boarded the train. The bar looked as if it had been hit by a pogrom. Then, to rub salt into the wound, the two policemen returned, threatening to fine the family for selling beer to soldiers, but they simply laughed and left without collecting the fine."

After Aranka got married in 1937, my grandfather was left working by himself in the restaurant. So, in 1938, my father quit his job in Budapest and went home to help him. But with only my father and grandfather left to run the restaurant, the business was getting very hard to maintain. The cost of hiring other workers was more than they could afford. So they sold the restaurant for 8,000 pengő[5]. I wonder if my grandfather had heard about the anti-Jewish decrees and decided to sell the restaurant while he still had the chance.

In the meantime, in light of the growing anti-Semitism across Europe, news of illegal Jewish immigration to *Eretz Yisrael* (the Land of Israel) spread quickly throughout Eastern Europe. My father's cousin, Gyula Kohn, who was an active member of the Zionist organization, Agudat Yisrael, had heard about an illegal ship that was to set sail for Palestine. Gyula convinced my father and Bözsi to seize the chance to flee Europe immediately, while they still could. Gyula made all the arrangements necessary to sign them up for the voyage.

The passengers had to pay for their own transportation. My father and Bözsi had 4,000 pengő all together for their tickets, but it was not enough to finance the trip. They needed to raise more money. Aranka had gotten married and 4,000 pengő of the money my grandfather had gotten from the sale of the restaurant was supposed to be for her dowry. But Gyula asked Aranka's parents-in-law (who were also his parents-in-law) to give up a part of the money in favor of helping to pay for the tickets. They gladly obliged. The Jews in Salgótarján also helped out, in addition to what their family could afford to pay.

Registration for the expedition, took place on 26 Király Street[6] in the Betar[7] office in Budapest. In 1939, my father's brother, Laci, traveled to Budapest to pay for the tickets. He had just received a visa for America. Aranka's husband, Laci (Aranka's first husband, and her brother, were both called Laci), would not leave his parents behind. My father asked his father to go with them to Palestine, "My father was around 60 and physically in good shape but he told me that he was already too old. I begged and begged my father to come with us. I told him that Laci could register him for the voyage as well. I was devastated and heartbroken. I had just lost my mother and did not want to lose my father as well. The hardest thing in the world was saying goodbye to him…"

My grandfather stayed in Hungary and went to Cserhátszentiván, where my father's aunt, Terry Klahr, lived. My father spoke about his

---

[5] The pengő (sometimes written as pengo or pengoe in English) was the currency of Hungary between January 1, 1927, when it replaced the korona, and July 31, 1946, when it was replaced by the forint.

[6] Lazar-Litai Haim AF- AL- PI SEFER ALIA B' Jabotinsky Institute, Tel Aviv, 1957.

[7] A Zionist youth movement founded in 1923 in Latvia by Ze'ev Jabotinsky.

Aunt Terry fondly, but with great sadness, "After I left Hungary, I never heard from them again. They were deported to Auschwitz with the rest of the family in 1944. Terry's son was also deported along with them. He was only 12 years old. Besides my father, I lost so many aunts, uncles, and cousins."

My father and his sister, Bözsi, and her family moved in with the Pragai family, until it was time to set sail for Palestine.

Terry and her son, Sanyi.

Wedding of Rözsi Kohn (my father's cousin) to Adolf Weiss, 1938, in front of my grandparents' restaurant.

Chapter 2

Escape to Palestine

Desperate to Leave Europe

With the persecution of Jews in Nazi Europe becoming intolerable in the 1930s, many Jews were increasingly desperate to leave. Avenues of escape were few since most countries closed their borders to Jews. Many Jews went to Palestine to escape Nazi persecution, but as their numbers grew, the British curtailed Jewish immigration, fearing Arab anger.

Thus, Aliyah Bet, or Illegal Immigration, which was called *ha'apalah* (the modern Hebrew name), was organized by several Jewish organizations to bring immigrants to Palestine. The Jewish immigrants were called the *ma'apilim*. During 1938-1939, many Jews often made the perilous journey by sea to Palestine in dangerous and overcrowded ships. Despite the risk, they preferred to try their luck in reaching Palestine rather than remaining in Nazi Europe.

British navy boats patrolled the shores of Palestine to prevent the *ma'apilim* from landing. Arrangements were made ahead of time for the ships to land at secluded beaches in the hope of eluding capture by the British. Immigrants who were caught by the British were often taken to internment camps in Palestine or turned away completely.

The *Sakarya*, with 2,300 passengers, was one of the largest *ha'apalah* ships to reach the shores of Palestine illegally. It consisted of a convoy of Jews from three ships that carried 2,300 Jews: the *Spyroula*, the *Saturnus*, and the *Grein*.[8]

It was the *Grein* that transported the Hungarian Jews to Sulina, Romania, where they eventually boarded the *Sakarya*. Romania, in 1939, had a relatively lenient attitude towards Jews, and basically turned

---

[8] Lazar-Litai Haim AF- AL- PI SEFER ALIA B' Jabotinsky Institute, Tel Aviv, 1957.

a blind eye to the illegal immigration of European Jews to Palestine from its territory.[9]

One of the major problems facing the organizers of the *Sakarya* expedition was the demand that Jewish immigrants have an "End Visa" to "their country of destiny"[10]. So the ship's organizers bribed officials in other countries to issue what they called a "collective visa", permitting a large group of people (according to a submitted list of names) to enter a specific country. The Romanian officials then issued transit visas to the people on the list, even though they were well aware that the Jews never intended to go to that country.[11] My father's Hungarian passport shows the "visa" he received to Liberia.

Forged visa to Liberia.

---

[9] Eri Jabotinsky, "The Sakarya Expedition", Manuscript (Jabotinsky Institute Website, A4 – 8/5).

[10] Eri Jabotinsky, "The Sakarya Expedition", Manuscript (Jabotinsky Institute Website, A4 – 8/5).

[11] Eri Jabotinsky, "The Sakarya Expedition", Manuscript (Jabotinsky Institute Website, A4 – 8/5).

Making Their Way to Sulina, Romania

On November 1, 1939, the first group of 800 Czech *ma'apilim* left Prague for Sulina, Romania and sailed down the Danube River on the *Saturnus*. In Romania on November 10th, the second group of 500 immigrants boarded the Romanian barge, *Spyrola*, also bound for Sulina.[12]

The Spyroula[13].

---

[12] "Forty Years Ago on the Frozen Danube" - story of the Sakarya. Excerpted from a forthcoming book, 1979 by Yitzhak ben Ami. Jabotinsky Institute Website, K6 /4/14/1.

[13] Courtesy of the Jabotinsky Institute in Israel.

When the transports reached Sulina, there was no ship waiting for them. There were 1,300 people floating down the Danube with winter approaching and the real chance that the *ma'apilim* would freeze or starve to death. But the Nazis had threatened that if they did not leave immediately, they would all be sent to the Lublin concentration camp[14]. The choice was taking a risk at sea or facing certain death in Nazi Europe. All opted for a chance to survive.[15]

With the coming of sub-zero temperatures and freezing waters, a sea-bound vessel that would take them to Eretz Yisrael had to be found urgently. Betar activists Eri Jabotinsky[16], Faltin[17], Eliyahu Glezer[18], and Dr. Willy Perl[19], all instrumental in organizing the expedition, intensified their efforts and finally located a Turkish ship, the *Sakarya*, which would take them there. The *Sakarya*, according to the contract signed with its owners, was supposed to arrive during the third week of November.[20]

By the time the *Spyrola* reached Sulina on November 22, the *Saturnus* had already arrived, but the *Sakarya* was nowhere to be seen. Both the immigrants who were stranded in Sulina awaiting the ship, and the organizers of the expedition, sat through weeks of desperation, hoping the boat would eventually come. On December 10th, the *Sakarya* finally arrived at Sulina, 23 days behind schedule.[21]

The *Sakarya* was a Turkish-owned, 3000 ton coal ship unfit for transporting passengers. Every inch of the ship was covered with a thick layer of coal dust. There were only remnants of cabins. Her three bunkers were only accessible by steep and dangerous ladders and there was no light. It needed to be converted into a ship that could accommodate 2,300 Jewish illegal immigrants. The organizers wanted

---

[14] A German concentration camp located on the outskirts of Lublin, Poland during WWII.

[15] Lazar-Litai Haim AF- AL- PI SEFER ALIA B' Jabotinsky Institute, Tel Aviv, 1957.

[16] Eri Jabotinsky, son of Ze'ev Jabotinsky, was a member of the Revisionism's Betar youth movement. He was instrumental in coordinating illegal Jewish immigration to Palestine.

[17] Faltin was instrumental in the ultimate success of the Sakarya expedition.

[18] Head of the Czechoslovakian Betar movement.

[19] A Viennese lawyer, longtime Betar member. He was involved in arranging for the evacuation of European Jews by sending them to Palestine during the Nazi occupation of Europe.

[20] Lazar-Litai Haim AF- AL- PI SEFER ALIA B' Jabotinsky Institute, Tel Aviv, 1957.

[21] Lazar-Litai Haim AF- AL- PI SEFER ALIA B' Jabotinsky Institute, Tel Aviv, 1957.

to immediately begin building bathrooms, stairways, kitchens, and bunks, but the owners would not agree until every legal detail was covered and the money paid.[22]

Weeks of blackmail, which were referred to as "negotiations", began between the two Turkish owners, Avni and Kemal Bey, and the *Sakarya* organizers. The initial agreement was a payment of £6,750 for transporting 900 immigrants to Palestine. By the time the *Saturnus* and *Spyroula* arrived, there were 1,300 people. So, they raised their price to £12,000. The owners refused to allow any immigrants to board the *Sakarya* without payment. In order to raise money, the ship's organizers decided to take another transport of Jews from Budapest. When the owners heard this, they raised their price to £17,500.[23]

So through the joint efforts of Irgun[24] activist Dr. Reuben Hecht[25], and Agudat Yisrael, another transport of 200 Viennese and 400 Hungarian *ma'apilim* was organized to join the *Sakarya* expedition. They chartered a boat called the *Grein*. Among the passengers on the *Grein* was Dov Gruner, the Irgun activist who was hanged by the British in 1947.

---

[22] Eri Jabotinsky, "The Sakarya Expedition", Manuscript (Jabotinsky Institute Website, A4 – 8/5).

[23] Eri Jabotinsky, "The Sakarya Expedition", Manuscript (Jabotinsky Institute Website, A4 – 8/5).

[24] A Zionist military organization that operated in Palestine during the British mandate in Palestine. The Irgun was instrumental in helping to organize illegal immigration from Europe to Palestine.

[25] A wealthy Swiss national who helped many Jews reach Palestine illegally.

The Grein Arrives in Budapest

On Friday, December 24th 1939, the *Grein* arrived in Budapest with 200 Viennese Jews already on board. About one third of the immigrants belonged to Agudat Yisrael and the rest to Betar. In order to prevent desecration of Shabbat, the Agudat Yisrael people boarded during the day. The others boarded at night.

Getting a permit to leave Budapest involved great difficulty since there was a fear that the Danube River might freeze on the way. Dr. Willy Perl, who arrived from Zurich to Budapest, called the German transportation authorities[26] and told them that the meteorological station in Romania had just informed him that temperatures in Romania were going to rise in the following two weeks so there would be no danger of the river freezing. Dr. Perl was asked to sign a statement saying that he would be personally responsible for the veracity of this statement. After Dr. Perl signed, the *Grein* was given permission to leave Budapest. Even before the *Grein* set sail six hours later, Dr. Perl was already on his way back to Zurich. A few days later, the *Grein* arrived at Sulina from Budapest and was frozen solid in the ice overnight.[27]

My father: "We were staying with the Pragai family until it was time to go to sail. We had to be ready to go as soon as we got notice. I left Budapest with Bözsi, her husband, and their two children, Malka and Cippora, Friday, December 24, 1939."

"The boat left Budapest on the Danube River and we went through Yugoslavia. I remember Yugoslavia well. The Yugoslav Jews welcomed us over there. We passed through different ports and the last stop was in Sulina, Romania. We stayed there for more than six weeks. We stopped

---

[26] At that point, the Germans were still allowing Jews to leave Europe.

[27] Eri Jabotinsky, "The Sakarya Expedition", Manuscript (Jabotinsky Institute Website, A4 – 8/5).

there. Why did we stop? I did not know at that time that the money we paid was just for the trip to Salina. It wasn't for the trip to Palestine. We had to wait six weeks until the money was collected to pay for the rest of the journey. The conditions on the ship were very bad. There was no heating. It was winter time and it was below 32 degrees Fahrenheit. It was very cold, but we survived. We had a kitchen there run by Jewish people."

Malka: "We boarded a boat one Friday night in December, 1939. All we were allowed to take with us was a knapsack. Even I had a small one. We had some cans of sardines and even that the Hungarians took away. In the boat there were small cabins with two berths which were for the women and children. My mother, my sister, and I had the bottom berth and on top was a mother with two boys. We sailed down the Danube towards the Black Sea and the port town of Sulina in Romania. When we reached Sulina, we got stuck at the port of Sulina for a month and a half. We were not allowed to leave the boat. On January 19th, I had my seventh birthday and Uncle Gyuri[28] appeared with a piece of cake all covered with cream. I do not know where he got it."

The *Grein* sailed from Budapest on December 24th. There were now 1,900 *ma'apilim* heading down the Danube, or anchored in Sulina. Another 400 Polish and Romanian Jews managed to reach Sulina and were allowed to join the *Sakarya* expedition. The number of *ma'apilim* now reached 2,300.[29]

Weeks were spent trying to squeeze as much money as they could out of the Jewish immigrants. They had to come up with the money before they would allow the *Sakarya* to leave.

---

[28] Uncle Gyuri is what all of my father's nephews and nieces called him.
[29] Eri Jabotinsky, "The Sakarya Expedition", Manuscript (Jabotinsky Institute Website, A4 – 8/5).

The Grein, the boat that took the Budapest transport to Sulina[30].

Waiting to Sail

It took until the middle of January to come up with the money needed to continue the journey to Palestine. Eri Jabotinsky went to Bucharest and desperately sent cables and made phone calls to the entire Betar organization, primarily to the representatives in New York. To meet these payments, most funds were contributed by the British, South African and Romanian Jewish communities, and additional funds were transferred from Budapest on behalf of the *Grein* group. The American Friends of Jewish Palestine donated the final £500 which enabled the *Sakarya* to set them free of the owners' clutches. [31]

In the meantime, the *Saturnus ma'apilim* were on board a German vessel flying the swastika, captained by a Nazi. Towards the end of December, he informed the passengers that his orders were to return to Austria, before the freezing of the river set in, with or without his passengers. The two Turkish owners agreed to allow the 800 immigrants on the *Saturnus* to board the *Sakarya*. The *Saturnus* went out to sea, came alongside the *Sakarya* and the immigrants crossed over onto it on a plank.

A few days later, as the temperature continued to drop, the river froze and the *Spyroula* was slowly turning into a block of ice as the temperature dipped well below zero, seriously threatening the lives of the immigrants. So they had to hire another ship with a heating system, the *Stefano*, and transfer all the *Spyroula ma'apilim* aboard. This saved the lives of the passengers. [32]

---

[31] Eri Jabotinsky, "The Sakarya Expedition", Manuscript (Jabotinsky Institute Website, A4 – 8/5).

[32] Eri Jabotinsky, "The Sakarya Expedition", Manuscript (Jabotinsky Institute Website, A4 – 8/5).

In the meantime, the *Sakarya* entered the Danube canal and tied up at Sulina wharf. They started fixing up the *Sakarya*, building bunks, kitchens, bathrooms, and access stairways to accommodate the passengers on their journey.

Leaving Sulina

By mid January, they had raised most of the money asked for by the *Sakarya* owners. The *Grein* people and about 400 additional immigrants were the last to board[33].

My father: "At the beginning of February, around midnight, we boarded a smaller boat that took us to the Black Sea. There, we were transferred to a Turkish ship, a coal ship, called the *Sakarya*. The departure was on the open sea. We boarded by climbing a very long and loose ladder. Erno, Bözsi's husband, carried his older daughter, Malka, and I carried Cippora, his younger daughter, to the deck of the ship. We were 2,300 refugees. I have to mention that life for me on the boat was very interesting. It was the first time I had seen Jews from all over Europe; there were Jews from Austria, Czechoslovakia, Romania, and Yugoslavia."

Malka: "Then on a cold night, approximately six weeks after we had arrived to Sulina, we sailed to the *Sakarya* in small boats. We had to climb up a rope ladder with the sea under us. It was a miracle that nobody fell into the water. It was a coal cargo ship. Inside there was a big space and shelves around where the families settled. There were no windows, no air, and very little space. My mother was seasick all the time but my father, Uncle Gyuri, and I were on the top deck, which was not a very safe place because it was not fenced in."

---

[33] Eri Jabotinsky, "The Sakarya Expedition", Manuscript (Jabotinsky Institute Website, A4 – 8/5).

Finally at Sea

There were about 200 additional passengers gathered on the dock during the last hours, begging to be let aboard. The *Sakarya's* owners refused. As the *Sakarya* finally sailed away, on February 1st, the last thing the *ma'apilim* saw were several hundred shivering people standing on the pier, some crying and some stony-faced, left behind, knowing certain death awaited them.[34]

My father: "We left Sulina. After a couple of days, we sailed down the Black Sea and reached Istanbul. We moved on to Gallipoli in the Dardanelles Strait[35] where we stayed for a few days. Then we continued our journey to Palestine. But just after we passed through the Dardanelles Strait, we saw a British ship approaching our boat. They ordered us to stop. The British soldiers boarded our ship and took it over. Armed British soldiers remained on the *Sakarya* till we reached Haifa."

Malka: "The captain tried to get away, but the British fired a shot over the ship and he stopped the ship. All the passengers ran to the side where the British were and the ship almost turned over. The British soldiers boarded the boat. We, the children, received delicious chocolate so we were very happy to see the British when they boarded. The British asked the leaders of the expedition what had taken so long, for they knew even before we left Sulina, that we were on the way to Palestine, and were waiting for us."

---

[34] Eri Jabotinsky, "The Sakarya Expedition", Manuscript (Jabotinsky Institute Website, A4 – 8/5).

[35] A narrow strait in northwestern Turkey connecting the Aegean Sea to the Sea of Marmara.

Descent on stairs to lower deck of the Sakarya,
illegal immigrants' sleeping quarters.

On the deck of the Sakarya.

Ma'apilim on the deck of the Sakarya gaze at the
sunrise at the entrance of the Dardanelles Strait[36].

---

[36] All three pictures on this page are courtesy of the Jabotinsky Institute, Tel Aviv,
Israel.

Ma'apilim on the deck of the Sakarya, which flies
the Turkish flag, approaches Haifa port.

Spotting a British warship from the Sakarya.

View of approaching boat with British soldiers,
from the deck of the Sakarya[37].

---

[37] All three pictures on this page are courtesy of the Jabotinsky Institute, Tel Aviv,
Israel.

Imprisonment at the Atlit Detention Camp

The *Sakarya* arrived in Palestine on February 13, 1940. The passengers were very lucky the British let them continue to Haifa. In many cases the British turned ships with illegal immigrants back to Europe. When they arrived in Haifa, the immigrants were removed from the ship and detained by the British in the Atlit detention camp[38].

First the married and old people were taken to Atlit. The young men, including my father, were kept on the ship for another three weeks. By the time they were allowed to leave the ship, they were full of lice. They were taken to a container where they were able to clean off the lice and then sent to Atlit to join the rest of the *Sakarya* passengers. "One distinct memory I had", my father recalled, "was seeing the Italians bombing the refineries in Haifa while we were interned in Atlit".

Altogether, they were held there for six months, from February to August. On Aug 12, 1940, Tisha B'Av[39], everyone from the *Sakarya* was freed. Bözsi, her husband Erno, and their daughters, Malka and Cippora, went to live in Petach Tikva. My father went to Jerusalem where he spent three years. The first thing he did was to go to the Kotel (Western Wall)[40] to pray.

---

[38] The Atlit detention camp was established by the British as a detention camp, south of Haifa, for illegal Jewish immigrants who tried to enter Palestine between 1939 and 1945.

[39] A date on which many calamities befell the Jewish people, among them the destruction of the First and Second Temples.

[40] The Western Wall is a surviving remnant of the Second Temple, which was destroyed by the Romans in 70 CE.

My parents in Atlit, 2006.

Bözsi (Elisabeth) and her husband Erno's names appear on the original passenger list of the Sakarya. (Courtesy of the Jabotinsky Institute, Tel Aviv, Israel.)

A list of some of the Sakarya passengers (including my father's name) recorded by the Jewish Agency. At the top it says, "A list of Jewish immigrants who came to Eretz Yisrael. The ma'apilim from the ship Sakarya, arrived February 14, 1940, released from Atlit August 12, 1940". [41]

---

[41] Courtesy of the Central Zionist Archives, Jerusalem, Israel, ISA1\15491\3.

Tragedy Back Home

In 1944, after the Nazis invaded Hungary, they started rounding up the Hungarian Jews and confining them to ghettos from where they would be transported to concentration camps. Ghettos were areas inside certain towns and cities that were designated as "exclusively Jewish".

One of those Jewish ghettos was created in Szécsény. Two blocks around the synagogue were closed off and declared the "Jewish zone". Between May 5th and May 10th, 1944, the Nazis gathered Jewish communities from several towns surrounding Szécsény and transferred them to the Szécsény ghetto. Once there, all their money and jewelry were confiscated. If someone was suspected of not handing over all their valuables, they would be taken to the local public school and tortured by the gendarmes[42]. At the beginning of June, the Jews from the Szécsény ghetto were taken to Velics-major, a farm in the area used to place the Jews until they were taken to their next destination. Between June 10th and June 12th, they were herded into cattle cars from Velics-major and taken to Balassagyarmat. From there, they were deported to Auschwitz[43].

Another Jewish ghetto was established by the Nazis in Salgótarján. My father's sister, Aranka, my grandfather, and the rest of their extended family, were all rounded up and sent there. On June 12, 1944, the Jews in the Salgótarján ghetto were taken to the railway station for deportation to Auschwitz. It was there that my father's Aunt Hermina, and her husband, Lajos, were shot right in front of their children, Eva and Magda.

---

[42] Hungarian policemen that were sent to round up the Jews.
[43] A magyarországi holokauszt földrajzi enciklopédiája. Randolph L. Braham, ed. (Budapest: Park Könyvkiadó, 2007), p. 779-800.

When they reached Auschwitz, Joseph Mengele[44] stood there to "greet" the Jews and decide which one was to live and which to die. Aranka's face was always plump and full of color while Eva's was always pale. Mengele sent Eva and her sister Magda to the line designated for the people to be murdered in the gas chambers. Aranka was sent to the line for those going to work. On the spur of the moment, without a second thought, and without thinking of the consequences to herself, Aranka grabbed Eva and pulled her over to the line on which she was standing. This saved Eva's life. During their time at Auschwitz, Aranka was always the stronger one. She often gave any extra scraps of food to Eva, even if it meant getting beaten for it.

Eva's sister Magda was also selected to be exterminated. Eva tried to save her, but was not successful. Magda died in the gas chambers and Eva was devastated after failing to save her. Seeing her parents murdered in front of her eyes, and losing her sister, Magda, was too much for Eva to bear. She remained heartbroken for the rest of her life and was never able to speak about what she went through.

When Eva's daughters, Chana and Orly, were teenagers, they asked their mother to tell them something about her sister, Magda. Eva remembered with great sorrow that Magda was a gifted poet and wrote especially about Eretz Yisrael. She said, "Magda was very quiet, but had the gift of being able to powerfully express the passions that lay hidden inside her inner world."

It reminded me so much of my father, so quiet, but so spiritually powerful. I often wonder whether my father and Magda ever spoke about their passion for poetry during those Shabbat meals they ate together in Salgótarján.

Very few members of the family returned from Auschwitz. My father's sister, Aranka, survived together with Hermina's daughter, Eva, as well as Perla Weiss (wife of Nachman Zvi Haupt) and her daughter, Ibi.

---

[44] A notoriously, cruel SS officer and physician who sent millions of Jews to their death in the gas chambers at Auschwitz. He also performed inhuman medical experiments on the Jewish prisoners.

Eva Klein, 1948.

Aunt Hermina.

Shlomo Haupt, My Father's Cousin

My father's cousin, Shlomo Haupt, was the son of Nachman Zvi Haupt (Cippora Haupt's brother) and Perla Weiss. Shlomo was born in the town of Cserhátszentiván[45], Hungary. At the age of six, his family moved to Pásztó.

Just prior to the summer of 1944, in accordance with new anti-Jewish laws passed in Hungry, Shlomo was drafted into a Hungarian forced labor camp in Jósva, Hungary, working for the Hungarian military. In July, the camp officially closed. Shlomo, along with other Jewish survivors in the camp, were crammed into cattle cars and locked inside for five days until they reached Stanislavov, Poland.

The Jewish laborers were brought to the front between the Russian and the German/Hungarian forces to build a new defense line. They were used in the construction of a barbed wire fence between the two armies. The Jews worked under constant gunfire from the Russians and were also forced to clear minefields in the area. Many laborers were injured and killed as a result.

In September, Shlomo's battalion was taken to a section of the Prut River, approximately 200 kilometers from the Hungarian border, where they were ordered to build a bridge for the German army. The physical labor was excruciating and they were forced to work from inside the river's freezing waters.

At one point, Shlomo and the other Jewish prisoners in the battalion were handed over to the Germans. Their food rations slightly improved, but the Germans required a better effort on their part in return for receiving more food. If the prisoners did not complete their assignments

---

[45] Situated approximately 91 kilometers (56 miles) from Budapest.

on time, they were severely punished. The physical labor was so brutal that many people just collapsed and died from exhaustion. Their battalion consisted of between 200-240 Jews. Many of the prisoners were above sixty years old and the younger prisoners tried to do much of the work for the older ones.

All the prisoners contracted diarrhea after drinking from the river. The doctors among them suggested they use charcoal or drink Turkish coffee as a cure.

They were then marched for five days, walking up to seventeen hours a day to Bershka, Poland, approximately 300 kilometers away. There they were forced to unload heavy weaponry from the train station.

In the fall of 1944, the prisoners transported heavy weapons on wagons up the Carpathian Mountains for six weeks. But instead of using horses, the order was to harness the Jews to the wagons. They had to do difficult physical work in the cold and the rain and they suffered greatly. All the prisoners were infested with lice that permeated every pore of their bodies.

At the end of fall, 1944, they returned to Hungary and were once again under the command of the Hungarian military. In October, when Miklós Horthy, the Regent of Hungary, was deposed from power, the Hungarian army crumbled. This meant that each prisoner was at the mercy of his own platoon leader. Shlomo's platoon leader was a drunkard who stole the prisoners' money and attempted to rape them. The Jewish prisoners fled for their lives. Shlomo and two of his friends reached the area of Gyöngyös, where they hid in a corn field.

There they were caught by a German army unit and the commanding officer ordered one of his soldiers to return them to the Hungarian army platoon where they were to be executed. But since there were no Hungarian army units in the area, the German commander ordered the execution of Shlomo and his two friends. A German soldier told them to hand over any money they had and then ordered Shlomo and his friends to start walking in front of him in the direction of the river. When they reached the river, the German soldier shouted that he was going to shoot them. At that moment, Shlomo and his friends jumped into the river, the soldier shot into the air, and they made their escape.

They made their way in the direction of Nagymaros. At that point in the war, the Russian army had reached Hungary and Shlomo was forced to work with the Russian army (a Ukrainian unit). The Russians needed manpower to help with the war effort. So they would forcibly recruit every able-bodied man they came across in every village they passed through and use them for transporting heavy weapons. After a day's work, the laborers would run away so the Russians would simply go to the next village and gather another group of men. Shlomo was one of the few men that actually remained with the Russian army unit and he was treated relatively well until they reached about 15-20 kilometers from his home town of Pásztó.

Until then, the Russians did not know that he was Jewish but the people from Pásztó did. Once the Russians discovered he was Jewish, their attitude suddenly changed for the worse and Shlomo knew he had to flee. From the backpack which he had kept under his bed he took only his *Tefillin* (phylacteries)[46] and his precious family photo album. He left everything else behind. He told the soldiers that he was going to the woods to gather wood for a fire and ran for his life.

On the way to his home town of Pásztó, he came across a disgruntled, drunken Russian soldier standing on a bridge, firing his gun in all directions. Some Hungarian soldiers in the area managed to restrain him. The Hungarians did not speak a word of Russian and the Russian did not speak a word of Hungarian. After being with the Russian army for a few weeks, Shlomo had picked up a couple of words in Russian and asked him what he wanted. The Russian soldier was overjoyed to hear someone speaking Russian. He said that he had been injured, was hospitalized in a hospital in Pásztó, and then was sent back to his unit. Shlomo continued to speak to him and was somehow able to calm him down. This allowed Shlomo and the other soldiers in the area to escape.

Shlomo reached his home in Pásztó at the beginning of January, 1945 and found that the Russians were using his house as a makeshift hospital. He simply hung around and started to help them in any way he could. He did not tell them who he was. They were just happy that someone was assisting. That same evening, an order was given for the Russians to vacate the hospital and move on.

Shlomo then traveled to Budapest and worked relentlessly to provide food for the Jewish concentration camp survivors that started trickling back. In May, he received word that his sister Ibi (Malka) and his

---

[46] A pair of black leather boxes, worn by observant Jews, containing parchment scrolls inscribed with passages from the Torah.

mother had been liberated from Auschwitz, but unfortunately his father had been murdered in the gas chambers.

In June he started to work with Jewish organizations that helped bring Jewish refugees from the DP (displaced persons) camps to Palestine, known as *Aliyah Bet*. In two years, he helped over 30,000 Holocaust survivors reach the shores of Eretz Yisrael. In 1948, Shlomo, his mother, and his sister finally left Hungary for Palestine, where they went to live in Safed, in northern Israel.

Front row, (l-r): Ibi Haupt Greenbaum, her mother, Perla Haupt.
Back row, (l-r): Laci Greenbaum (Ibi's husband), Shlomo Haupt.

Aranka Klein Feuerstein, My Father's Sister

After liberation from Auschwitz, Aranka returned to Salgótarján, where she had been living with her husband, Laci Feuerstein, before the war. Unfortunately, she found out that he had been murdered.

There, she met her cousin, Gyula Kohn, whose wife and two children had perished in Auschwitz. After a short while, Gyula and Aranka decided to marry. They re-opened the motel and restaurant "Badacsony" that had belonged to Gyula's parents-in-law (Rachel Lea and Avraham Yitzhak Adolf Feuerstein) before the war.

They remained in Salgótarján until Aranka became pregnant. They decided that they did not want to raise their child in a place where they had both suffered so much. They also did not want to remain under Communist rule. So, at the beginning of 1947 they left Hungary and went to Sweden where they stayed with Gyula's sister, Ilonka Kohn Hertz, and her husband, Jenő Hertz, in their apartment in Stockholm. Aranka gave birth to their daughter, Mary, in Sweden in October, 1947.

In the meantime, Aranka had written to her brother Laci who was already in America, saying that they wanted to immigrate to the United States. Laci immediately arranged for their immigration papers and became their American sponsor. They arrived in New York in 1950.

In front of the motel and restaurant "Badacsony", approximately
1939. (l-r): Two policemen, unknown girl, Gyula Kohn, unknown
woman, Ancsi Feuerstein, rest are unknown.

Ilonka's apartment in Sweden, 1949.
Front row (l-r): Gyula Kohn, Klari
(Béla Kohn's wife – Béla was Gyula's brother), Mary, Aranka.
Back row, standing: Ilonka Kohn Hertz (Gyula's sister).

Life in Palestine

After being released from the Atlit detention camp, my father went to Jerusalem with some friends he had become acquainted with on the boat. He stayed in Jerusalem for nearly three years. He took whatever job he could find, starting out as a dishwasher in a restaurant, and then in the Eden Hotel. Then he worked in a factory making metal parts for hand grenades for the British army.

His yearning for his parents grew, and for the rest of the family he had left behind in Europe. His mother had already died and he had no information about his father. He used his writing as a means of coping with the profound sadness and grief that had overtaken his life. He felt the emotional need to put down in writing the outpouring of his feelings of longing. It seems to me that his writing became his refuge.

In the following poem, the earliest one he wrote, my father expresses the pain of losing his mother at such a young age as well as the "raging storm" (the war) which forced his family to disperse. He ends on a note of optimism and hope for the future that some day, the war will end and better times will come.

Jerusalem

November 19th, 1940

The Great Storm

You were the crown of your tree and you held your head high among your branches. Your sprouts reciprocated the care they got from you with joy. But you left us so young, dried out before it was your time, you left your sprouts to the mercy of the wind.

The raging storm smote your trunk to death, scattered your branches around. They are looking for each other now, standing in the freezing cold, like a frozen man behind a barricade of ice.

The storm is raging ever so violently around him, cracking the vulnerable branches into pieces. And then it quiets down and they rest a bit in the shade. But some inner rain chases them ahead and it does not let them rest in a stranger's land.

Go away, it's cold here too and you will not find a warm place. And the branches would run again in search of each other. But the storm approaches, again, throwing (deep) obstacles in their way as if fate didn't want them to succeed. The branches tire out on their aimless way and bow to their unchanging fate.

They wait and wait until everything goes silent, the storm has to cease at one point. The branches got stronger and they are budding again. The leaves are swaying sadly, mourning the winter. When will you be together again, and recall old memories of the times when you were resting under the crown that cared for you during all those times? It is all just a dream now, it's impossible for it to come true. Give up what passed, turn to the future. Maybe it will compensate you for the terrible mistakes of the past.

Settling in Palestine

After settling in Petach Tikva, Erno, Bözsi's husband, eventually joined the British army and served for four years. Following his three years in Jerusalem, my father went to Tel Aviv to learn the diamond trade. He worked as a diamond cutter for close to a year in Netanya.

He stayed in Netanya during the week, where he lived in a dilapidated shack. There was a bed there but no finished floor. Instead, there was just sand everywhere. For Shabbat, he would go to Petach Tikva and rent a room close to his sister, Bözsi. After they arrived in Palestine, Bözsi's third child Simcha (Simmi) was born. Malka, Cippora, and Simmi would always be anxiously waiting outside their house for Uncle Gyuri to come because he would always bring some special treat for them. On Sunday he went back to work.

In the evenings in Netanya, he spent much time playing chess with his friends. His brother Laci had taught him to play chess in Hungary and he learned to love the game very much. He eventually continued playing chess with his children, grandchildren and great-grandchildren.

In the meantime, feeling very much alone and missing Laci who he had been so close with, my father decided to apply for a visa to join him in the United States.

My father, with his friends in Palestine.

My father, working as a diamond cutter in Netanya.

In Petach Tikva, Bözsi stands next to my father with
her children, Cippora (left) and Malka (right).

Joining the Palestinian Jewish Coast Guard

Throughout his stay in Palestine, my father was constantly looking for information about the fate of his father and the rest of his family that had remained in Europe. Later when he spoke about the war, he described how little he really knew until the war ended.

"We did not get much information about what was happening in Europe at the time. The newspapers in Palestine talked about the European Jews being deported, but until 1945, it remained more of a rumor than anything. On one occasion, Bözsi received a post card from Aranka, sent by her from Auschwitz[47]. This instilled great fear in me that the rumors of the mass murders might really be true."

"I never stopped worrying about my family. I so desperately wanted to get information about what was happening in Europe that, despite my fears, I even thought of joining the Jewish Brigade[48]. When I mentioned to Bözsi that I was thinking about joining the Jewish Brigade, she started crying and begged me not to go. So I decided to join the *Mishmar Hayam* (the coast guard). That was around 1944, and I was there for about a year and a half."

With heart-wrenching honesty, my father expresses his guilt for saving himself while millions of others were dying. In his poetry, he so candidly admits how scared he was of fighting in battle and even questions whether he had a Jewish heart or soul.

---

[47] After the Jews reached Auschwitz, many were handed postcards with a uniform message indicating that they were in good health and that things were "going well with their resettlement". The Nazis encouraged the deportees to send these postcards to friends and family as a way of deflecting the reports of the systematic extermination of the Jews in the concentration camps.

[48] A brigade of Jewish volunteers that was sent to Italy to fight the Germans in 1944.

Netanya

January 2nd, 1944

As you can see I haven't escaped. I could be surrounded by the pleasant smell of the palm trees of Southern Italy, I could be enjoying the charming melody of the Italian language, could be admiring the achievements of Italian art.

I could be in Rome – and just to not forget us, Jews – be checking out Michelangelo's world famous work, Moses, that shows this man's hard features, his extraordinary determination (I have seen it on photos before). It allows one to peek over, to the other world and steal a look at its human guardians, who looks just like someone from the 20th century. But I'm a coward, I ran away, afraid that I will be hurt there.

I got scared by the whistling bullets,
And the cries of the vulnerable souls,
And I covered my ears,
Not to see, not to feel,
What do I care what happens over there,
What do I have to do with the death of millions,
Sooner or later they would all pass,
As a small human, what do you care
Live for yourself, don't mind the rest.
Why should I be different from the tree
That blooms just like before
Even though the trees around have fallen,
It rattles its leaves, this is its goodbye
I'm off to whip the others,
To wake up the humans inside.
Since they are still almost wholes
They haven't lost parts of theirs.
But me – I'm covered by insects,
I'm wounded
I am slowly going numb.
Who knows if I will ever be healthy again.

Even if we learn our times,
Will we ever be brave and strong as we were
Will we ever be ready for a new life
If after all this, I am sitting here,
If help I cannot offer
I could deliver a hit myself –
Even if the second bullet will end me too.
But as I wrote to you in the first part
I am a coward and nothing else.
I am coming up with terrible tales to save my soul,
There is no Jewish heart, no Jewish soul in me.
Will you ever understand,
That these excuses are facts.
How I sell myself and my character
For naught; fatherly or brotherly love.

Patrolling the Shores of Haifa

In his interview, my father describes his work in the coast guard. "I was a policeman working for the coast guard which was under the control of the British army. Our job was to patrol a 15 kilometer strip from Haifa to Atlit. Clandestinely, we also did work for the Hagana[49] (the Hebrew word for "defense")."

My father, during his stint in the coast guard patrols the shores of Haifa, 1945.

---

[49] The Jewish paramilitary organization that defended the Jewish communities of pre-state Israel during the British Mandate of Palestine from 1920 to 1948.

"I belonged to the HaPoel HaMizrachi[50] unit of the Hagana. The work we did for the Hagana was illegal at that time. One of the reasons I joined was that I was hoping to get information about the fate of my father and my family from the people coming from Europe by boat."

"In 1945, I remember when Russian prisoners of war who were liberated by the British were brought to Israel and then sent back home. My thoughts never left my father. I was praying that I would find my father among the prisoners. But, I never did find him. I never saw him again."

"It was at that point that information about what really happened during the war started trickling in. We used to go some nights to lectures where we were getting more and more news. We started hearing about the mass murders but we had such a hard time accepting it. We did not want to believe it."

In the following excerpt, my father writes about the news that the Palestinian Jewish Shore Guard was going to be dismantled.

Haifa

February 11th, 1944

A seemingly insignificant, unverified piece of information appeared among the lazy company and spread fast along the dirty halls of the barracks. Obviously the boring monotony of this new life has not yet broken these youth down. They were truly interested in the topic, each and every one of them. Many raised an eyebrow when first hearing about the dismantling of the unit guarding the shoreline; others looked up to the skies for the new turn of events.

In the hardly functioning theater club, the failure of which can be blamed on the boring nature of police work, the news became the primary topic of the day. Our philosophers, who cannot be simply contented with merely acknowledging certain events, following some preliminary diplomatic negotiations, reached the conclusion that the case is not as simple as many think. The Palestinian

---

[50] A religious Zionist pioneering and labor movement in Eretz Yisrael.

Jewish Shore Guard carried out its task faithfully even in the direst of times, when Rommel[51] was standing at El-Alamein. Even then, the soldiers were relentless.

The whole affair seems to be a bit ridiculous today, one has to admit since we are talking about a fairly small group that could have lost - or been victorious for that matter – along with the international protectors of the Mediterranean.

Two years have passed since, and the guards are still there, on the sea shore or among the beautiful trees of the Carmel in Haifa. But let me continue my accounts – following the meeting of our diplomats they began to speculate about the future task of the unit, coming up with their own prophecies, since nobody received any official notification about our present and future mission. As is well known, the leaders of the three great powers are planning our future while learning from the experiences of the past. The creators of this war will take on the mission and will make sure that such "system errors" cannot happen again.

As it is obvious the sudden disbanding of our coast guards is directly related to the recent negotiations of the three great men. The news is not yet good, but it's obvious that the decision about us was made in a certain harbor at the Black Sea. As we heard there is a program that will make sure that those who participated in the victory will get their new positions in the new world to come.

Needless to say it would be outrageously unjust if our unit couldn't represent itself at the world conference. According to certain news, we will be tasked to participate in international security situations and we are expecting the invitation for the peace conference without much excitement. I just want to draw my company's attention to one thing. We all need to represent

---

[51] During WWII, when the Nazi forces under General Field Marshal Erwin Rommel were moving towards Egypt and Israel, they had plans to set up an extermination camp like Auschwitz in the Dotan Valley had the Germans broken through Egypt. Fortunately, Rommel was defeated in the summer of 1942 at El Alamein. The Dotan Valley is mentioned in the Bible as the site where Joseph was sold by his brothers.

the same, strong viewpoint so when the English diplomats will do their best to satisfy the Arab diplomats, our legendary guards won't be separated once they cross to Europe to participate in watching over the enemy states.

Following the dismantling of my father's coast guard unit, he went back to work as a diamond cutter.

My Father's Writings from March, 1944 – May, 1945

In the following diary excerpt, my father depicts a magical, wintry day.

Petach Tiqwa

March 4th, 1944

A painting of the village!

It is a tough, cold winter. The sun left us to visit other parts of the world. The street is deserted and quiet. Nothing disturbs the wintery silence. All around, the fields are white. Wherever you look that is all one can see. Hearing bells from the distance I look out through the thick window. A horse passes by, a sleigh after it. How wonderful it is to see this magical journey. I can see a man wrapped in fur in the carriage, in a warm hat and high boots. Around noon the winter seems to relent. The sun rises from behind the valley. The street is not silent anymore – due to the bells and the wonderful fights of an army of children.

As if they were on the battle field they stand up in a straight line, ready to shoot with their snowballs. The fight starts after the whistle of the referee. The sound of snowballs cracking in the cold winter night made the fight exciting.

From the skating rink one can hear the happy notes of jazz, skating couples draw arches on the ice. The noise from the mountains is getting louder and louder, sleds are gliding in the valley. From time to time a scream pierces through the landscape, the rider of an overturned sled shouts. In the evening hours the fields are silent again, daytime is taken over by the long winter evening. There is merry singing around the fireplace, men smoking pipes play cards. The army of the house has turned in, as they turn in for a night's rest.

In the following poem, my father uses vivid imagery to describe Moses receiving the Torah at Mount Sinai, and Moses' desire to see the Land of Israel after G-d tells him he cannot enter the land.

Petach Tiqwa

March 17th, 1944

Moyshe, Moyshe go up with the people
Show them the way towards Zion
Lead your people with the fire of your torches
The day becomes night and then dawn
Moyshe becomes furious, angry
He passes his black tablet to the "Am[52]".
He looks up to the unseen annoyed
With tears glittering in his eyes
He throws himself to the ground of the meadow
But his eyes look up, to the sky,
He turns back towards the fields of Mitzrayim[53],
He thinks of the lands of the Eretz[54] with an aching heart.
Moyshe calls to himself the eldest of the people
To tell him about the plans of the Lord,
Because I fought for countless years
Leading the people out through the great desert.
Now that I reached the gates of Zion
And I bow myself at the foot of the hill,
If I could just see Eretz Yisrael
I would happily fall into the arms of death.

[52] The people of Israel.
[53] "Egypt" in Hebrew.
[54] The land of Israel.

And Moyshe hears a sound
The Lord is speaking to him
Put on your sandals
And be ready to part
You can see over there
Mount Sinai
You can see from there
The meadows of Eretz
Moyshe's heart is full
with desire and thankfulness
He reaches up
Murmuring a prayer.
When reaching
The mount of Sinai
He looks deep
into the midst of the valley
The sun rises
Above the mountains
His staff in his hand
He walks amid the new valleys.

In the following, my father explains that although changing one's opinion is viewed as hypocritical in other people's eyes, he was not afraid to reconsider previous viewpoints.

Haifa

July 18th, 1944.

The passing of doubts!

Charged with hypocrisy I had to put down what I think. Every change in my opinion comes after a certain pressure, the apparent beauty or interesting nature of a new thing that necessitates the revisiting of the previous idea. Every person, depending on his age, wits and experiences might encounter such a revolutionary change – which feels absolutely natural to him while encountering the disapproval, pity or animosity of others. I would like to respond to my prosecutors, I would like to explain that it is not hypocrisy to change my clothes to assure a certain financial situation and I show a different face as my situation demands it – thus selling myself and my character. Even if I seem to be hypocritical when taking someone else's habits into consideration I will still stand for the same things, and I rightly admit that what seems to be my hypocrisy is nothing else but the respect I show for others' traditions.

In this excerpt of his diary, my father expresses his own feminist views.

Haifa

December 19th, 1944

Invitation for a name day[55]

Not that it was ever a habit of mine to celebrate names- or birthdays. There has never been any special ceremony at these occasions in my family. It was only my late mother's birthday we celebrated with loving kisses. My birthdays were never mentioned. Maybe this means I'm modest. Not that I don't value myself according to my abilities and humble knowledge - which I try to determine according to my objective criticism. I haven't celebrated these days of mine because they just weren't special occasions. Firstly, I would like to apologize if I disturbed you with these sentences. You might be surprised that I took the occasion of your birthday as an excuse to write to you – despite the fact that I just told you that I don't put emphasis on days like this. Needless to say, this is a compliment to you - not that this was the intended tone of my

---

[55] Nameday is a tradition celebrated in Hungary in which one's first name is associated with a particular day of the year. On that day, people for whom that day is named are usually wished a "Happy Name Day" and receive gifts from well-wishers.

letter. By the way, the only way I know how to give compliments is the objective way.

Apart from the fact that the subject of the letter is quite timely due to your fast approaching birthday, apart from that, I also feel it is my friendly duty to write to you. If you don't approve of this latter excuse, that will not change my standpoint.

What does one wish for a girl (maiden)? First of all I wish you thought about this day, the starting day of the best year of your life. The 21st year is the most beautiful, unrepeatable time, especially in the life of a girl (maiden). I think, I can value this day of yours even more than you do, since I know that after this short period of entering life one notices with disgust its not-so-ideal ways, its shortcomings and its far from perfect nature – just like the others living on the face of the Earth.

I don't wish you such experiences at such a young age. Abroad we used to wish girls a handsome husband, a happy life, and – maybe not even as a joke – a dozen children. Of course abroad we did have the financial means to accomplish all this. I am absolutely in agreement with the first two wishes but I am wishing for a reduction with the third – because of two reasons. All mothers' natural wish is to have an offspring, which ideally makes her life pleasant, gives one a goal, ambition. But this shouldn't mean that one doesn't have other goals in life, that one shouldn't find joy in herself or in her environment. One also has to know how to be selfish. Not to mention that the delivery of every child endangers the life of the mother. How could one demand such a brutal thing? Is a husband allowed to demand his wife to risk her own life? There is only one situation in one should have a child – if the woman wants an offspring at any price.

It seems like the evolution of culture harms humankind. I think this is a fact. I disapprove of men who overlook such a thing and don't recognize this special task of the woman. You know me and my democratic views – I demand the full recognition of women in the name of humanity. In connection with this I have to mention the especially risqué position of girls. I would like to point out one of the shortcomings and unfairness of this crazy world. Why does the male world demand full chastity, purity from the woman while men are walking knee deep in sin? Why is one allowed or not allowed to do the same as the other? I wonder if women haven't grown to understand this. Is this why they are not fighting for their equality? The will, the pride is missing from you, when it is about the fight for your human rights. I remember you asked me once if I would marry a girl who had had intimate relationships with men before. I said no. Needless to say this answer does not reflect my point of view. It never did, I just didn't want you to know so you wouldn't judge me.

I'm not being too focused today – completely diverted from my subject. How many kids do you want? Please, think it over and don't give an easy answer – that you want 2 or 3 kids, because I just might answer that I wish to have exactly as many houses in Tel Aviv as you will have after those 2 or 3. I saw mathematicians make mistakes! As the saying goes; "Don't tolerate the Tot[56], he will push you out of his house. It means that if you let him do something, he will have endless demands. I hope you won't use this same answer on me now that I invite you to celebrate your birthday. Unfortunately I won't have you in my shiny castle where black clad waiters serve you the espresso, fruits etc. But I promise you that as soon as I will be able to do so, I will send my four-in-hand[57] for you. I hope you will understand my joking/playful tone but I certainly hope this won't be an obstacle and we will meet up to celebrate this day, which – as you know – is my birthday too.

In the following excerpt, my father philosophizes about socialism.

January 26th, 1945

The necessary control of human freedom

According to my beliefs human rights stand above all. I believe in unlimited freedom – in the framework of Socialism, of course.

---

[56] The translator was unsure of what my father meant by the word Tot.

[57] A kind of horse drawn carriage.

Naturally this means that the following should not be included: free trade, financial speculations, the dissemination of nationalist ideas, etc. - all the things allowed by a liberal world view.

Yes, I would like to renege on what I said before. I do think that human freedom has to be restricted. First it might look like the violation of human rights, but it is useful and in the best interest of humankind, used only to show the way to a world where one can live, breathe and work freely, where one's safety, a calm atmosphere, a life without troubles, the improvement of humankind, moral purity is ensured, where people, families can live a happy life.

This way we might avoid the tragedy of humankind, this way we won't use humans as live bullets in a war for an ideal that is so not practical, that was proved to be a failure by history. It brought along the death and suffering of millions upon millions throughout the past thousands of years – while not achieving the one thing that is craved for: peace and happiness. But the damn liberal spirit managed to achieve one thing; it managed to mislead humankind and convince him with a certain financial sacrifice – which itself was produced by the sweat and blood of the people. They gave them guns, inciting the less enlightened people to kill his brother, mother, father just so his own son will survive - or die by the murderous dagger of his own neighbor, brother, for the liberal ideas.

Back to my subject – why do we need to control human freedom until humankind finds its world stone/world circle? Until then – we can say – we live in chaos where all kinds of different beliefs are advertised, the people is confused by all the different voices. It is easy to mislead them like this, to abuse their weakness in a time when they are selfish and confused.

It is without a doubt that Marx's ideas will have to fight a dual of life or death for humankind and it is without a doubt that those representing the liberal ideas will not be deterred by anything in order to implement their system. It is unquestionable that the Socialist idea is gaining respect and power, and the time will come when it will fight its final battle with liberalism, the belief that is still supported by part of the people who serve as mercenaries to its means.

Even if through blood but it has to happen and then in the newly cleansed atmosphere the people can be taught and informed, the new generations raised with this new idea. And when the last servants of the evil spirit have died all the control – that now seems to be the violation of human freedom – can be relinquished.

In this excerpt of his diary, my father wonders about the woman he will marry. The part where my father says that he is "about to get married", is more wishful thinking at this point. The "new stage in life" he is talking about is the stage in which he starts looking for his bride and he feels that he will find her soon.

Netanya,

May 5th 1945

Letter to an old friend

I'm writing to you from my new home, sitting next to a steaming cup of tea on a quiet evening. I'm writing to you about my new place, the new stages of my life etc. As you know after finishing my glorious career with the police in Haifa, the ending of which was duly celebrated by a small company of friends, I returned to diamond cutting. After some initial difficulties I managed to find a home, but only in a "shack".

But never mind, it's not important – although I'm about to get married. Other than the unimportant technical issues one more serious affair is in the way of my nuptial - other than that you can wish me good luck. Unfortunately I cannot tell you more about my bride. Where is she, how is she? It is very possible that she already exists and is suckling sweet milk from her mother's breast or is happily dancing the waltz, held passionately by another man.

After the first difficulties with my job I am on my way to the right path and I'm happy to announce that I'm making a pound a day. Naturally, this is the smallest possible salary, but I am slowly getting ahead, head first. Now I can feel the astounding difference between my life in Haifa and now. It was worth choosing this, more troubled path – my rest after a day's work is truly peaceful and I enjoy Shabbat more etc. I find my job interesting and it does not bore me at the least, on the contrary – the hours fly by. From time to time I bump into a stone that is more difficult to work with or on nicer days I have to duck under the desk to look for stones that fell from the bench. The work is actually so tiresome that I cannot go on with the high life I led in Haifa, which I don't even miss so much. But let me stop my chatter now. I wish good luck to you, the new bride. Greetings to your girlfriends, especially to the loud one I ran into in Haifa once. I hope he gave my greetings to you.

With friendly regards…

Leaving for America

In the meantime, the American consulate called my father to tell him that his quota number had come up and he was issued a visa for the United States. He left Palestine in August, 1946 to join his brother, Laci, in America. First, he went by ship to Marseille, France.

When he got to France, he needed a travel document and was told to go to the police department in Paris. After showing them his American visa, they provided him with a permit to remain in France until November 30.

From there he was supposed to go to New York. But at that time, there was a massive wave of labor strikes spanning numerous industries. Among them, the longshoremen were on strike. Not only could he not reach New York, but the whole Atlantic Ocean was closed down. No ship came or went. My father finally found a French ship that was traveling to the United States, the *S.S. Formaulhaut*. The destination was originally supposed to be New York, but the longshoremen strike spread and both the East and West Coasts were shut down. So the ship made its way to Vancouver, Canada.

This was my father's last diary entry.

Baranquilla, Columbia

October 22nd 1946

It is a pity that we have such sad moments in life. Human life is so short – we shouldn't allow ourselves to have unpleasant minutes and hours.

I am a truly sentimental man with extreme mood swings. The events around me are pushing me from one extreme to the other – sometimes I must look truly childish. I am not trying to find excuses, and I definitely don't need to defend myself. I also think this is still better than the opposite – although my character has caused me to have quite unpleasant minutes which could act as warnings. Without any interest to further analyze the causes and see if its roots lie in weak nerves I have just one concern – I wonder if I will ever find someone who will satisfy this sensitivity in a marriage.

As the maritime strike continued, he was stranded in Canada. He then contacted his brother, Laci, who was already living in New York. Due to a U.S. immigration restriction, his point of entry to the United States was supposed to be only from San Francisco so he couldn't go by train to San Francisco. In addition, he was traveling on an expired passport.

His Unites States entry permit was due to expire December 7, 1946 and as of November, 1946, he was still stuck in Canada. My father was becoming extremely concerned, so he contacted a journalist from the Vancouver News Herald, hoping that if the story hit the papers, it might help him out.

My father's predicament reported in a newspaper.[58]

He then contacted HIAS (Hebrew Immigrant Aid Society), an organization that helped Jewish refugees, and they came through for him! In November 1946, almost five months after he left Palestine, he

---

[58] Material republished with the express permission of: **Vancouver News Herald**, a division of Postmedia Network Inc.

was finally informed that he had been granted a new visa with which he could enter the United States from Vancouver.

On November 20, 1946, my father finally entered the United States through Blaine, Washington. He traveled by train to New York, which took about three and a half days. When he finally reached New York, Laci and his wife, Ancsi, were there to welcome him.

When asked what his thoughts were about finally reaching America, he said, "My life had started anew in the United States but I missed the Jewish life I had in Israel and vowed that one day I would return to Eretz Yisrael. Meantime, I became acquainted with my wife, Olga, which brought a welcome change to my life."

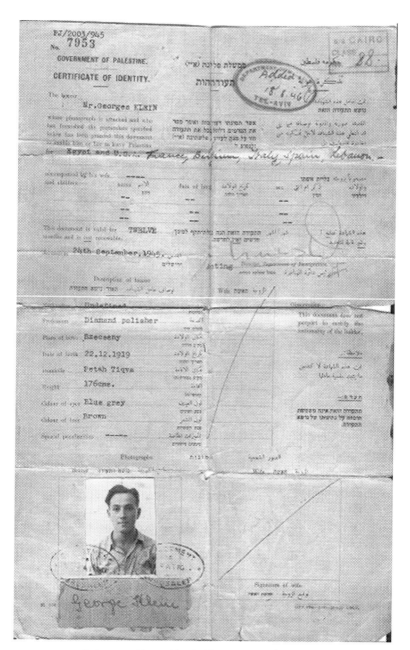

A document issued by the Government of Palestine
enabling my father to leave Palestine.

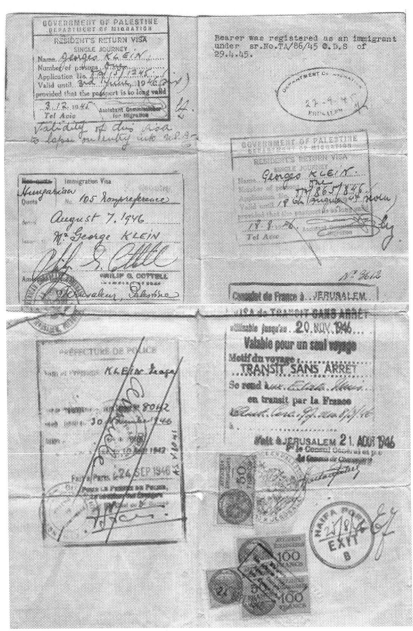

On the back of the document enabling my father to
leave Palestine are the visas and the exit stamp.

Document of arrival to Marseille, France; document allowing
my father to remain in France until November 30, 1946.

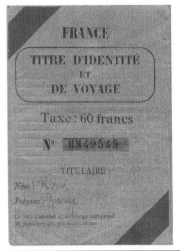

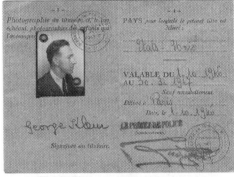

A travel document my father received from French authorities.

On the ship from France to Canada, 1946.

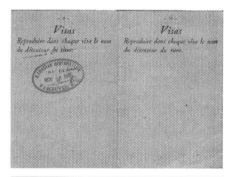

New travel visa from the Canadian authorities issued November 15, 1946.
His visa shows the quota number he received for entering
the US. It was due to expire December 7, 1946.

A New Start in Life

On his arrival in the United States, my father moved into a one room apartment in Laci's house. Laci offered all his siblings a place in his house when they reached America. They all came to live at 312 West 105th Street in Manhattan.

Laci received his visa to the United States at the end of 1939. Kenny, Laci's son, calls this "a clear case of Divine Providence". He reminisces, "When my father was a medical student in Rome in the early-mid 1930s he passed by the American Embassy and decided, on a whim, to go in and register for possible immigration for himself and my mother. He did this for no particular reason other than maybe some day he would need it.... This was before the great danger to Jews became apparent. He subsequently forgot about the incident."

"Years later, when many people began to wake up to the danger in Europe, my father applied for a visa (in Budapest). By then, the list of applicants was very long and the clerk at the embassy was not optimistic that my father's application would be approved. However, the clerk had asked my father a question that jogged his memory about registering years earlier in Rome. This moved him and my mother from the back of the line to the very front and very possibly saved their lives. Had my father not decided to register when he passed the embassy in Rome I might never have been born. Once he reached the United States, my father was able to arrange for my mother, Ancsi, to come separately a year later in 1940."

Immigration to the United States in 1940 enabled Ancsi to escape the bitter fate that awaited the rest of her family. Her parents, Avraham Yitzhak and Rachel Lea Feuerstein, her sister Bluma, and Bluma's two children, Hava Malka and Menachem, were all deported to Auschwitz and murdered in the gas chambers. Her brother (also named Laci), was sent to a forced labor camp where he was beaten to death by Hungarian soldiers.

When Laci reached America, he was sponsored by Dr. Imre Braun, his cousin who had immigrated to America some years before. Laci and Ancsi went to live in Norfolk, Virginia. There, Laci completed the exams he needed for his medical license while Ancsi worked in a doll factory to support him. After Laci received his license, he worked as a resident physician at the US Naval Hospital.

It was during the time in Norfolk that they became American citizens and changed their family name to Kay since the name Klein sounded much too German and they did not want to be associated with anything German.

In 1942, they moved to New York and bought a five-story brownstone building on Manhattan's Upper West Side where Laci set up a private medical practice in his house. Their older son, Kenny, was born in 1943, and Stanley, their second child, was born in 1946.

When Aranka, her husband Gyula, and their daughter, Mary, immigrated to the United States in 1950, they also moved into Laci's house.

After my father arrived in New York, he found a job cutting stones for a diamond factory, and also met his first friend, Alex Taub.

Laci and Ancsi in Hungary before their marriage, approximately 1935.

Laci and Ancsi's wedding,
Hungary, 1936.

Laci and Ancsi stand in front of their five- story
brownstone on 105th Street in Manhattan, 1943.

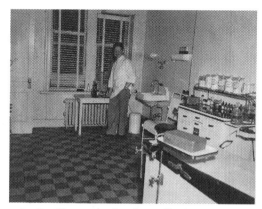

Laci's office on the first floor of his house, 1943.

My father, upon his arrival at Laci's house
sits with Laci's son, Kenny, 1946.

The waiting room in front of Laci's office, 1956.
Front (l-r): Gyula, Mary, Evelyn (my sister), my mother (holding me)
Back (l-r): Aranka, Laci, Kenny, Ancsi, Stanley, my father.

My Father's First Friend

The first friend my father made in the United States was Alex Sándor Taub, a Hungarian-born survivor. Alex was born on February 19, 1923 in Szamossályi, Hungry. In 1944, when Alex was 21 years old, he was drafted into *Munkaszolgálat*, the Hungarian Labor Army Camp in Kassa, Czechoslovakia. The men in this battalion worked clearing minefields barely surviving on meager food supplies.[59]

After approximately six months, they were forced to walk hundreds of miles to the Austrian/Hungarian border. Alex and many other Jewish prisoners were handed over to the *SS* (the squadron of Hitler's personal bodyguards). In January 1945, Alex was deported to *Schachendorf*, another forced labor camp in Austria, a subcamp of the Mathhausen concentration camp, where they were forced to dig trenches. Food and water were extremely scarce and people dropped off like flies. Alex became emaciated weighing a mere 80 pounds.

On March 28, 1945, two months after the Soviets invaded Budapest, *Schachendorf* was officially closed and the camp's survivors were gathered for a death march. Three days after all the prisoners were rounded up, Alex risked getting out of line to get some water from the camp's well. He tied a string he had found to a tin cup and lowered it into the well only to find that the well had gone dry. The day was very foggy and as he was walking back, he realized that the prisoners and the guards had already gone and he had been left behind. Alex had been saved from certain death.

Alex managed to make his way back to Budapest, part of the way on a Russian military truck, where he was directed to a local Jewish organization called *Bethlehem Gabor Tair*. They gave him food and put

---

[59] Lipiner, Michael. Magyar, Stars & Stripes: a Journey From Hungary Through the Holocaust and to New York. New York: iUniverse, 2005.

his clothes in a lice disinfecting machine. Then he was put in a bathtub and had his lice-ridden hair cut.

The next morning, he continued the journey to his hometown of *Szamossályi*, where he found that his brother Béla and sister Rózsi had returned from the war. Unfortunately, his parents and his brother Zoli did not survive.

In 1948, Alex emigrated to America, with the help of his Aunt Charlotte, his father's sister, who had already left for America in 1920.

Chapter 3

My Mother's Story

The Wrong Side

By Judy Cohen

In Auschwitz, there were two lines. The Jewish arrivals deemed fit to work stood on one line. The Jews standing on the other line, including the elderly, and women with children, were sent to the gas chambers. These lines in Auschwitz became a vision I have been unable to shake from my mind. Hearing my mother's testimony about her deportation to Auschwitz evoked in me the emotional need to describe what it was like for me "to see" the family I have always longed to meet standing on the wrong line.

Well, it's time to light again. I watch my mother as she slowly prepares the Yartzeit[60] candles. I asked her for whom she's lighting the candles. She names the members of her family for whose deaths she knows the precise date. She knows because in Auschwitz, they did not waste a second in slaughtering the ones that were not fit to work. Yes, she knows the precise date. It was the day they arrived in Auschwitz. It was the last time my mother laid her eyes upon the members of her family who were selected to stand on the other side. Only my mother and her sister Eva stood on the line which gave them the chance for life; provided, of course they somehow managed to overcome the hunger, sickness, and cold. My mother was strong enough to survive, but her younger sister, Eva, wasn't. She died three weeks after liberation. There are no graves my mother can visit but at least she knows when she can mourn them. The Nazis can never take that away from her.

But she cannot say the same for Zoli. Her brother Zoli had already been taken away to a labor camp a few years before. He never came back. She doesn't know when to light a candle for him.

---

[60] A memorial candle that is lit in memory of a dead relative.

My mother and Eva gazed across at the other line where the others stood for the last time. "I didn't know what was going to happen to them. I was so naive. Even after they were gone, we heard rumors in the camp about their fates, but I could not believe it. Who could have believed such a thing?" But her father knew. As soon as the cattle car which had transported them to Auschwitz crossed the border, my grandfather said to his wife, children and two grandchildren: "My loved ones, this is it". Yes, her father knew what was happening. And her sister Margaret knew too. When the cattle car in which they were deported pulled into Auschwitz, Margaret hugged her beautiful four-year-old daughter Susie and started crying. Yes, she knew too.

For me, you will forever be on that line. You will never move from there. You see, I don't want you to move. I want to forever remember you standing there, on the line. I don't want to remember what your last real moments were like; the unthinkable last moments when you were desperately gasping for breath[61]. I don't believe that such tormented souls could ever reach eternal peace.

They are there and I am always stretching my head out, looking from afar, searching for them among the people. They are there, on the line, suspended in time and forever imprinted in my memory. They will always be there, in the hope that I will one day be able to speak to them before they are taken away, always hoping that I might still be able to get to know them before they disappear.

They are all on the wrong side. Little Asher and little Susie are on the wrong side too. I see them all standing there on the other side and I want to scream out to them: "You're on the wrong side. Go to the other side, before it's too late." But they never seem to hear me.

You haven't heard me yet but you are all still there. So maybe, just maybe, one day you'll hear me and understand what I mean when I tell you that you should have been on the other side.

---

[61] Gas chambers were constructed at Auschwitz where more than a million Jews were murdered.

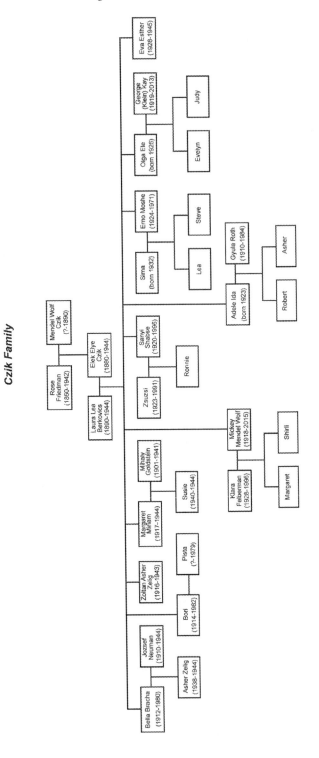

Rose Friedman's first marriage

Czik Family

The Czik Family

My mother, Olga Ele Kay, was born in Újfehértó[62], Hungary on July 3, 1926 to Elek Elye Czik (1880 – 1944) and Laura Lea Berkovics Czik (1890 – 1944). Elek and Laura were married in 1910. Elek Czik was the son of Mendel Wolf and Rose Czik (1864 – 1942). Mendel Wolf Czik died in 1890 when Elek was only ten years old.

Elek and Laura Czik had ten children:

Bella Bracha (1912-1980)
Bori Bila (1914 – 1981)
Zoltan Asher Zelig (1916 - approximately 1943)
Margaret Miriam (1917 - 1944)
Mickey Mendel Wolf (1918-2015)
Sanyi Shabse (1920 - 1996)
Adele Ida (born 1923)
Erno Moshe (1924 – 1971)
Olga Ele, my mother, (born 1926)
Eva Esther (1928-1945)

---

[62] Újfehértó (meaning "New White Lake") is situated in the Szabolcs county of Hungary, 122 miles east of Budapest. In April, 1944, Újfehértó had a population of approximately 2,500 Jews (about 400 families). Today, no Jews remain in Újfehértó.

Elek Czik, 25 years old.

Engagement of Elek Czik and Laura
Berkovics, Ujfehértó, 1910.

Front row (l-r): My grandmother Laura (pregnant with Eva), my mother (two years old)
sits on her lap, Adele, stands on the chair, my grandfather sits with Erno on his lap.
Back row, (l-r): Margaret, Bori, Bella, Zoli, Sanyi, Mickey.

Siblings of Laura Czik

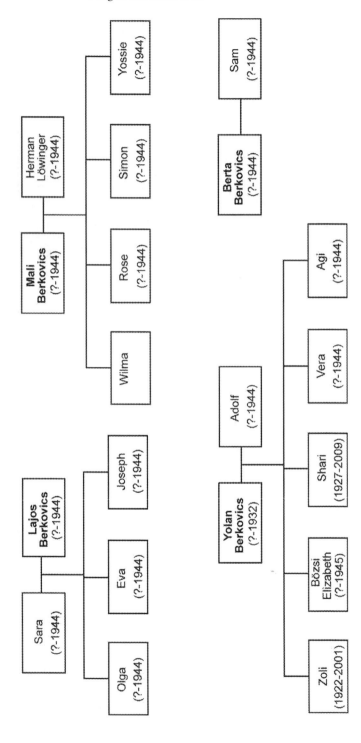

LAURA CZIK'S SIBLINGS

Laura Czik had four siblings:

Lajos married Sara and had three children, Olga, Eva, and Joseph. All perished in the war.

Mali married Herman Löwinger and had five children, Wilma, Rose, Simon, and Yossie. The entire family, except for Wilma, perished.

Yolan married Adolf and had five children, Zoli, Bözsi (Elizabeth), Shari, Vera, and Agi. Yolan died before the war, Zoli and Shari survived the war, but the rest of the family perished in Auschwitz.

Berta married Sam and both were murdered in Auschwitz.

Below is a photograph of Laura's brother, Lajos Berkovics. The photo was taken in 1929. Lajos gave the picture to Elek's sister, Pauline, before Pauline left for America.

Lajos Berkovics. The back of the photo says: Lots of love to Pauline.

Rose Friedman's second marriage

Dratler Family

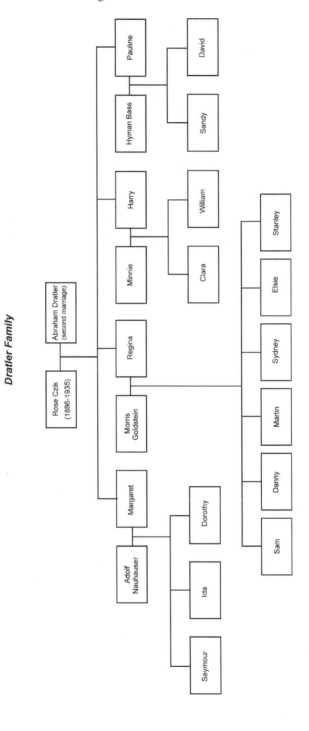

THE CZIK/DRATLER FAMILY

After Elek Czik's father, Mendel Wolf, passed away his mother, Rose, later married Abraham Dratler.

Rose and Abraham Dratler had four children:

Margaret married Adolf Nauhauser. They had three children; Seymour, Ida, and Dorothy

Regina married Morris Goldstein. They had six children; Sam, Danny, Martin, Sydney, Elsie and Stanley

Harry married Minnie. They had two children; Clara and William

Pauline married Hyman Bass. They had two children; Sandy and David

Rose and Abraham Dratler immigrated to the United States in the early 1900s with all their children except Elek, who had married Laura Berkovics in 1910. Elek always kept in touch with his family in the United States by mail.

Front (l-r): Elek's mother Rose and her husband Abraham Dratler. Back (l0r): Rose's twin sister Ida, Rose's daughter Pauline.

Pauline around 1925, Hungary.

Life in Újfehértó, Hungary

"We lived on a street which is now called Kossuth Ucca (pronounced "ootza", meaning "street" in Hungarian). I was one of ten children. It was a loving home. Our house was very small, but very beautiful. We used to have a beautiful garden with many different kinds of trees: peach, cherry, apple, plum, pear, and raspberry bushes. Their sweet fragrance would fill the air in springtime. I remember my father planting a walnut tree. It first bore fruit in 1943. We were only able to enjoy the walnut tree for a year, till 1944, when we were deported. My father was a skilled shoemaker and had a small shop about a half a mile away from where we lived."

"What I remember most was the wonderful relationship my parents had. I don't remember my parents ever quarreling. They had the utmost respect for each other and we, the children, had great respect for our parents. I remember that on Shabbat, my mother would always make sure there was not a sound in the house when my father took his afternoon nap."

"I grew up in a religious home. Every Friday evening, my father and brothers went to *shul* to *daven*[63]. My mother lit Shabbat candles and then my sisters and I would say prayers over the candles. On Shabbat morning, my parents went to *shul* with my brothers while the girls set the table for the Shabbat festive meal."

"Despite growing up in a very small house, we all had such a happy childhood. Looking back, part of the joys of having such a large family was sleeping in the same bed with my sister Adele. I remember walking to nursery school by myself at the age of five. When I was in first grade, my younger sister, Eva, started nursery school and I used to walk her there. We were only eighteen months apart and were so close."

---

[63] To pray, in Yiddish.

"All Jewish children in Újfehértó went to a Jewish elementary school where we studied secular subjects and learned to read and write Hebrew, as well as *daven*. I remember us singing "Hatikva[64]" (meaning "hope" in Hebrew) in Hungarian. We would also put on Chanukah[65] and Purim[66] plays. The school only went up to sixth grade. Those who wanted to provide a higher education for their children had to send their children outside of Újfehértó either to Nyíregyháza or Debrecen.

"After my siblings and I finished elementary school, my parents arranged for us to take apprenticeships under some of the local seamstresses and tailors and we all learned how to sew. I was an apprentice to Regina Kupferstein. Adele worked under Mrs. Gross, my sister Bori worked under Mr. Weisz, and my brother Mickey worked under Mr. Gelbman. My Uncle Lajos had a small clothing factory and I would make button holes for him. At home I used to love doing needlepoint and hand embroidery. Even after the war, those of us that survived remained in the needle trade. Two of my brothers, Mickey and Erno, had clothing factories in Montreal. My sister Adele's husband, Gyula, also had a clothing factory in Montreal. Gyula had lived in Újfehértó with his wife and two children until the Jews were deported in 1944. He survived the war but unfortunately his wife and children did not. My family and Gyula's family were very close. Gyula was an excellent tailor. I remember when he made a beautiful winter coat for my mother. My brother Sanyi was also an excellent tailor and worked in a clothing factory in New York after the war."

"We were ten children and we all had to help my parents. Thursday evenings I would help my mother bake *challah*[67] and coffee cake for Shabbat. Friday mornings I went to town to bring the *challah* and the coffee cake to the baker's oven. On Friday my mother prepared *cholent*[68],

---

[64] This was the anthem of the First Zionist Congress in 1897, and in 1948 it was adopted as Israel's anthem when it became a state in 1948.

[65] A Jewish holiday that commemorates the Jewish defeat over the Syrian Greeks (Seleucid Empire) who had tried to forcefully Hellenize them. When the Jews rededicated the holy Temple in Jerusalem and sought to light the Menorah, the oil that they needed to light the candles miraculously lasted for eight days even though they had only enough oil for one day.

[66] A Jewish holiday that commemorates the saving of the Jewish people in ancient Persia from Haman, who was planning to murder every Jew in one day.

[67] Special bread eaten on Shabbat and Jewish holidays.

[68] A traditional Jewish dish eaten for lunch on Shabbat.

which we took to the baker Friday afternoon. Since it is against Jewish law to cook on Shabbat, the cholent would sit in the heated oven from before sundown Friday (before Shabbat began) until the next day. On Saturday, just before my father and brothers came home from shul, my sisters and I would go to town and bring the cholent home."

"We also helped my mother with buying and cleaning poultry. After buying poultry at the local market, my mother would send my sisters and me to the *shochet*[69] to have the poultry slaughtered. After we brought the poultry home, we would help her pluck the feathers. Then my mother koshered the meat according to Jewish law. During the warmer weather, we would keep hens in a chicken coop we had in our back yard for egg-laying. Adele sometimes got very attached to the animals. One day, she found a small turkey that had apparently fallen off a cart taking animals to market. Adele brought it home, fed it, and nurtured it. The two became almost inseparable. The most amazing thing was that, every night, the turkey would cackle endlessly until Adele went to cover it. One day when Adele had returned home from somewhere, she went to the back yard to visit her turkey and became extremely concerned when she did not find it. She went inside the house and was horrified to see that my mother had just cooked it for dinner. Needless to say, Adele did not partake in the festive meal."

"For entertainment my sister Eva and I would sometimes go to the movie theatre. Every Saturday night they played Gypsy music in the town square. My friends and I would walk around and listen."

---

[69] A trained expert who slaughters poultry and other food permitted by Jewish law, according to the laws of kosher slaughter.

The Beginning of the Deportations

"Until the late 1930's, life was still pretty normal in Újfehértó. In the mid 1920s, my father decided that he wanted to join his siblings in the United States, who had all immigrated at the turn of the century. He called the American Embassy to inquire about getting a visa for his family. They told him that they would grant him a visa, but not for his wife or children. My father would never have considered leaving his family behind."

"By 1938, things took a turn for the worse. My oldest sister Bella got married in 1936 to Jozsef Neuman. They went to live in Sárospatak where they opened a business selling agricultural products. Their son, György Asher Zelig, was born in 1938. At the end of 1938, their business was confiscated and Bella's husband, Jozsef, was taken away to a forced labor camp, from which he never returned. Bella was left without a means of supporting herself and her child, so she brought her son, Asher, to our parents' house in Újfehértó and went to Budapest to work."

"My sister Margaret married Mihaly Goldstein in 1940 and went to live in Budapest. In 1941, while Margaret was expecting a child, Mihaly was rounded up by the Hungarian police along with other Jewish men, and taken to the Don River where they were killed. They were forced to stand by the edge of the river so that when they were shot their bodies would fall directly in. Immediately following her husband's death, Margaret returned to Újfehértó where she gave birth to their daughter Susie."

"In the late 1930s the Hungarian regime began to impose anti-Jewish laws and all Jewish males were forcibly conscripted into labor battalions for the Hungarian army. My brothers Zoli, Mickey, and

Sanyi were taken to forced labor camps. Once, in 1943, my parents got word that Sanyi was on a train that would pass through Újfehértó. My parents grabbed some food for him but by the time they got to the train station, the train had already left."

"My sisters Adele and Bori went to Budapest to work around 1943. They were both deported from Budapest to Ravensbruk concentration camp at the end of November, 1944. Bella was deported from Budapest a few days later at the beginning of December, 1944 and sent to Bergen-Belsen.

"On March 19, 1944, the Nazis marched into Újfehértó. A few days later, all Jews were ordered to wear a yellow Star of David on their clothes. The deportations in Újfehértó started April 15, 1944, the night Passover[70] ended. First they took away all professionals, such as doctors, soon to be followed by the rest of the town's Jews. That same evening, an announcement was made that all Jews were forbidden to leave their homes. Even as we were being taken from our homes, we still had not heard about the mass murder of Jews in concentration camps."

"We were taken from our home three days after the end of the Passover holiday, Tuesday, April 18, 1944. The gendarmes came to our house with bayonets and rifles and told us to take only what we could carry. We were allowed to take a change of clothing, a cover and a pillow. My sister Margaret naively asked if she could take with her a coat that her husband had given her. The sardonic reply was that they promised to send us the rest of our things later on. It was all very quick and we were out of the house in a few minutes."

"We were all gathered at City Hall. On the way, a young woman was so ecstatically happy that the Jews were being taken away that she started dancing with joy. There was one Jewish man who was very ill and could hardly walk. He asked to be taken in a carriage. The Nazi response was a cruel rebuff. I remember another mentally sick Jewish woman whom the Nazis handcuffed to her husband. We spent the entire day and night there. During the day, a city hall employee took information from each person, such as their name, and date and place of birth. That evening we were marched to the Simapuszta ghetto."

The Simapuszta ghetto had once been a warehouse for agricultural goods, including horse stables. The storage facilities were emptied out

---

[70] The Jewish holiday, which commemorates the exodus of the Jews from Egypt after 210 years in slavery.

and used as a ghetto to house the Jewish deportees from the nearby villages. The ghetto was surrounded by barbed wire and guarded by local police.

"We lived in animal stalls with meager rations. The police used different tactics to abuse us. I remember one day a policeman told a religious man to take out his tallit (a Jewish prayer shawl) and put it on the ground, and then he was forced to do pushups on it."

"While we were there, I remember seeing a man approach my father. The man obviously understood what was going to happen to us and offered to take Asher with him, but my father could not bear to part with his grandson. Looking back, I realize that Asher might have been saved. I never had the heart to tell Bella. I just couldn't."

"After four weeks in the Simapuszta ghetto, we were taken to the city of Nyíregyháza where we were crammed into empty apartments, stuffed like sardines in a can. This was to be the last stop before being transported to our final destination: the Auschwitz-Birkenau extermination camp."

"After ten days in Nyíregyháza, on May 22, 1944, we were loaded onto cattle cars. It was horrible. Inside the box cars, we were all jammed together. One bucket was placed inside for everyone, where we were forced to relieve ourselves in plain sight of everyone else. We were locked inside the cattle car for three days."

Margaret and her husband, Mihaly.

Bella and her husband
Jozsef, their son Asher.

In front of the Czik house in Újfehértó. (l-r): Bella's son
(Asher) in front of his mother Bella, their neighbors Boris
and Janos, Adele. Behind Adele stands Bori.

Arrival at Auschwitz

"As we crossed the Hungarian border, my father clearly understood what was about to happen and told us that there was no return from here. We arrived at Auschwitz on May 25, 1944. When the doors of the cattle cars opened, we were ordered off the train. I remember that I had wanted to take something of mine off the train, but my father just said to me very sadly, "You do not need to take anything. Just leave it. You will not need it here."

"After we got off, my family stood in a group and we were subjected to selection. A German officer came and motioned to my father to join a group of men on the left. After many years, I realized it was Joseph Mengele. My little sister, Eva, and I were motioned forward. As I turned, I saw my parents, Margaret, and the two children for the last time."

(l-r): Asher (Bella's son), my grandmother Laura, and Susie (Margaret's daughter).

Stripped and Shaved

"Eva and I were taken to a room with other women where we were stripped naked while soldiers watched. Our heads, along with every other body part were shaved. We were each given a dress to wear and then taken to barracks number 10. As I looked around, everybody around me resembled walking corpses. They looked like madmen, broken in spirit and body. I told my sister, 'You see! Everything will be all right! Look at all the crazy people. They are keeping them as well. I was referring to the starved prisoners that were already there. Eventually, we would look like just like them."

"Twice a day we were lined up and counted for hours. Then we went back to the wooden planks we slept on inside the bunker. Occasionally we were allowed to go out. When we heard airplanes, we would go out hoping they were Allied planes coming to liberate us. We were still alive and all we could do was hope. We were always hungry there. We were barely fed. The rations were meager; not enough to sustain us. We would get a watery soup with what I am sure had grass in it."

"When we were told that old, sick, and young people were sent to the gas chambers and cremated, we did not want to believe it. How could we believe it?"

Saved from Gassing

"My younger sister, Eva, was always the one to get hit by the guards. I did not think she would survive Auschwitz. One day there was a selection. Being selected meant being sent to the gas chambers. Even though Eva looked worse than I did, I was selected along with people from another group. We were forced to stand in one part of the yard. There were also another two sisters from our barracks. One was selected and one was not. When they allowed us to go to the washroom, my sister changed dresses with the other girl who was selected to be gassed and Eva came back to me. Even though it might have meant going to the gas chambers, the only thing then in our minds was that we wanted to stay together, no matter what the cost."

"That night, all those selected to die were put in a barracks. It was a horrible experience. Everyone was screaming and crying. It was so crowded that there was simply nowhere to sit. We managed to find a small spot somewhere, but there was only room enough for one person. Eva and I spent the night alternating sitting in that spot. There was simply nowhere else to sit. In the morning we were sent back to our barracks. I don't really know what happened; why we were not taken to the gas chambers. Everyone in our barracks was so happy that we returned. This was the first miracle which saved my life."

"We had to live with the daily horrors of Auschwitz. Electrocution and hanging were common forms of punishment. Auschwitz was surrounded by an electrically charged wire fence. One girl was thrown against the fence and was electrocuted. Her body was left there the whole day. Another time I saw three young men hanging. Their corpses were also left to hang for everyone to see. The Nazis often used this tactic as a way of intimidation and a warning of what would happen if we ever disobeyed. Once, when we were outside of our barracks, we saw a group of men who were forced to stand completely naked. When we saw them, we went inside so as not to embarrass them. I remember seeing that photograph in Yad Vashem.[71]"

"My sister Eva was already very sick in Auschwitz with constant diarrhea. She was very run down and didn't want to eat. I had to convince her to eat even the little food we got there."

---

[71] Israel's official memorial to the victims of the Holocaust

Kaufering Concentration Camp

"On July 29, the Ninth of the Jewish month of Av[72], three months after arriving in Auschwitz, Eva and I were taken to the Kaufering[73] concentration camp in Bavaria, Germany together with another group of women. The section of Kaufering we were in was probably used as a model camp to display to the world because we had a number of visits from the Red Cross. We lived there in earthen bunkers which were partially submerged. I remember that only the roof was above ground."

"We did several types of work. My sister Eva, as well as other young girls, worked in the private homes of the German officers. I had to clean the bark off of logs and then stack the logs in piles. Other times, I was sent to clean the barracks of the German soldiers. On Yom Kippur[74], about 20 of us were once taken to a farm and like good Jewish girls, we fasted. When the Germans found out, they told us that since we were able to fast a whole day, we wouldn't need our bread rations at night. Needless to say, we got nothing to eat that night."

"At Kaufering, Eva was very depressed. There, she would burst out, crying hysterically, and start banging her fists. Throughout the entire period we were in the camps, I constantly had to support my sister. She was very ill and I was always encouraging her not to lose hope."

"The second time my sister and I were saved came on the day there was an air raid and the farm where we were working was bombed. The Russian prisoners there were taken to the bunkers and the Jewish girls were taken to another building. The bunker took a direct hit and we girls came out without a scratch. This was the second miracle."

---

[72] A date on which many tragedies took place for the Jewish people, among them the destruction of the two Holy Temples.

[73] A subsidiary camp of the Dachau concentration camp.

[74] The Jewish day of atonement on which Jewish people fast.

"The third miracle also happened in Kaufering. One time, I was told to take some food to the house of a German officer. By the time I came back, I was already late for roll call. The women there were gesturing that I should rush back before the Germans found out that I was not standing there with everyone else. I saw a guard aiming his gun at me. I was terrified. I started to run back as fast as I could and all I could think about was my sister Eva. She was already so ill. What would she do without me? He cocked his gun, pointed it in my direction and pulled the trigger. He missed. Then he lowered the gun and let me join the others. Afterwards, I started wondering why the guard did not shoot me. They didn't need a reason to shoot people there."

Transferred to Bergen-Belsen Concentration Camp

"At the end of November, the camp was evacuated and we were all transported to Bergen-Belsen by cattle car in which we sat on the floor. The ride took about twenty-four hours. In Bergen-Belsen, we had to get up at 6:00 am every morning for roll call. We had to stand there for hours each time, no matter what the weather was like. The barracks we were in was overcrowded and filthy. There were no gas chambers there but we were all being systematically killed by starvation and disease."

"On December 25, another transport arrived. Eva and I both hoped that we would see someone there who had information about what happened to our other sisters. Suddenly, Eva let out a scream as we saw our oldest sister Bella getting out of the cattle car. We screamed with happiness when we saw each other because we were still alive but saddened by the fact that little Asher, our sister Margaret and her daughter Susie, and our parents, were dead."

"She looked horrible. She had been locked up in the train for three weeks. She was deported from Budapest on Dec. 8, 1944 and arrived in Bergen-Belsen on Dec. 25, her birthday. She looked so bad that we hardly recognized her. She came with her beautiful *siddur* (a Jewish prayer book) that her husband had given her, and her pocketbook. In her pocketbook, she had a few photographs of her dear son Asher, the only remnants she had left from him. Unfortunately, they took her beautiful *siddur* but somehow they let her keep her pocketbook. She was able to keep the photographs of her beloved son throughout her incarceration in the death camp."

"Then a few days later, more transports arrived and on one of them was my beautiful cousin Elizabeth. Again, we were happy to meet another relative. Unfortunately she soon became very sick and died on March 11, 1945 in Bella's arms, just prior to liberation.

"At times, we were taken to the forest and told to collect wood. Every time we were told to collect wood, there was one German soldier who always beat me. One time he beat me so hard that it left marks on my back. Life was becoming worse and worse. It was winter and it was very cold and snowy. We had no stockings and were given only one dress to wear. We were made to stand outside for hours in the freezing cold."

Bella's son, Asher, in front of his grandparent's house in Ujfehértó.

My mother's cousin, Bözsi Elizabeth Weiss.

Liberation

"Towards the end of March, the shooting began; a sign that liberation was near. By this time, we were hardly getting any food. There were days in which we got no food at all. We were all just lying on the floor. One by one, the girls were just not waking up anymore. We were so sick that some of us were unable to move. We all had diarrhea and we could not make it to the pails. We were all dying. Eva was especially ill."

"A few days before liberation, the shooting intensified. At one point, one shot entered the barracks and hit a woman inside. She was there with her sister, who happened to be a doctor, but she was unable to save her. We were all just lying there waiting, with the dead among us."

"Then one day the shooting stopped. An English soldier appeared at the door waving a white flag. He told us that we were being liberated and we would all be fine. That was April 15, 1945. After the British soldiers came, I remember that the German camp personnel were forced to remove the corpses and clean out the filth from the latrines. After a few days, we were all deloused. They poured a white powder on us and the lice just poured off of us. We were all infested. At one point I went to the storage room where the food was kept to see if I could get more food. As I got close to the entrance, I just collapsed because I was so weak. I crawled to the wall and had to push up against it to get myself back on my feet. I returned without any food."

"While we were still in Bergen-Belsen, we were cleaned and wrapped in blankets. We were then taken to another building; a clinic of some sort. Bella and I were taken to the attic and those who were sicker than us were kept downstairs. As people died and beds were vacated, people from the attic were taken downstairs. The sicker ones, like my sister Eva, were kept downstairs. At that point we still had not received clothes and still only had a blanket to cover us."

"Bella and I would go downstairs to visit Eva. One day someone came up to the attic to tell us that our dear Eva had asked to see us. We immediately went down to see her, but by the time we reached her, she was no more. I thought she might be cold and I wanted to cover her, but someone sadly told me that she no longer needed a blanket. We were too weak to ask where she was buried, but we did learn that the people that died there afterwards were buried in separate graves. We weighed about twenty-six kilos when we were liberated."

"Eva succumbed to her illness three weeks after liberation in 1945. We were so close and I miss her terribly. We had only one photo of Eva; one that had been sent to our relatives in the United States before the war."

Front, (l-r): Adele (standing), Eva and my mother (sitting). Back, (l-r): Sanyi, Bori, Grandmother Laura, Grandfather Elek holding Asher, Bella's son. In the background are the grape vines that grew in front of their house in Újfehértó.

Taken to Sweden

In 1945, after the liberation of the concentration camps, Sweden received thousands of Holocaust survivors and provided medical treatment. My mother and Bella were just two of the survivors who were treated there.

"Four weeks later, after we were finally able to walk, the Swedish government arranged for us to travel to Sweden to receive medical care."

"First we traveled by train to Lübeck, Germany. I remember that on the train we received some chocolate and thought it was the best tasting chocolate I had ever eaten. Looking back, it was probably just an ordinary piece of chocolate!"

"From Lübeck, we traveled to Sweden by boat. We arrived June 16, 1945 at Gothenburg, Sweden. At this point, we did not know whether anyone else from our immediate family was still alive."

"We were taken to Lund, located in the province of Scania. They converted part of Lund University to a hospital to accommodate the concentration camp survivors that were brought there. We were treated very well by the doctors and nurses. After a while, we started regaining our strength and gaining weight."

"Later on, we were taken to convalescent homes in Loka Brunn and Katrineholm. While we were still in Loka Brunn, we received a letter from Adele, Bori, and Mickey saying they had survived the war and returned to Újfehértó where they met."

"In Sweden, efforts were made to find relatives that may have survived the Holocaust. Ads were placed in the newspapers to help locate the missing relatives of Holocaust survivors. Lists of survivors and their whereabouts were also read on public radio broadcasts. I remember hearing my name on the radio. People from HIAS (Hebrew Immigrant Aid Society) came around to all the survivors and asked if we had any relatives in the United States. My father's mother and his siblings, one brother and three sisters, had all immigrated to the United States in the early 1900s. I said that all I knew was my uncle's name Harry Dratler, who resided in Brooklyn. I told him that I did not have an address. The HIAS representative said that was probably sufficient to find him." And it was!

"A neighbor of my uncle's happened to see his name in the newspaper and told him that someone was looking for him. When he looked at the ad, he recognized my name, Olga Czik."

"He sent us a telegram saying that he would immediately start to work on arranging the legal papers needed for us to join them in the United States. In the meantime, we corresponded with Aunt Margaret and her other siblings and they sent us care packages."

"Eventually my sister Bella and I recovered and we started to work in Mjölby. We spent altogether a year and a half there making children's sports clothes at a factory. We lived in apartments that were actually part of the factory complex. That was the last place we were in Sweden. We worked there for about ten months from March, 1946 until January 1947."

My mother's employer at Mjölby met her and Bella at the train they were taking to the Port of Gothenburg, where they would board a ship to America. He presented a certificate of excellence to my mother to show his appreciation for the work she did at his factory.

"After arranging for the official documents needed for their immigration to the United States, Aunt Margaret, Aunt Pauline, and Uncle Harry paid for our passage (boat fare was $300 per person). They each paid $200."

My mother and Bella traveled to the United States for ten days on board the *SS Drottningholm*, a repatriation ship that was used to exchange prisoners of war, diplomats, women and children, between the warring nations during World War II. How fitting that this would be the ship to take my mother and her sister Bella, to the place where they would be starting their life anew.

Concentration camp survivors stand in front of Lund University (converted to a hospital), August 1945. Third row from bottom: Bella is the sixth person from the left. My mother stands directly in back of her in a white blouse.

This photo of my mother and Bella was sent to Aunt Margaret from Katrineholm in 1945. My mother is still very thin here as she had not yet gained her full weight back yet. It says: "Lots of love to Aunt Margaret and family".

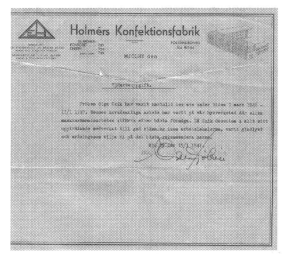

A letter of reference given to my mother in praise of the excellent
work she did at the factory. The letter also praises her for
contributing to the positive atmosphere at the workplace.

Passport issued to my mother by the
Hungarian authorities in Stockholm.

(l-r) Bella, my mother, in
Loka Brunn, January, 1945.

What Happened to the Family During the War

Bella

Bella's husband Jozsef Neuman was deported to a forced labor camp and never returned. Their son, Asher, was murdered in the gas chambers of Auschwitz. Bella was deported to Bergen-Belsen in 1944 and was liberated in April, 1945. She immigrated together with my mother to the Unites States in 1947.

Margaret

Margaret's husband, Mihaly, was taken to a forced labor camp and then murdered by the Hungarian police. Margaret and her daughter, Susie, were deported to Auschwitz in 1944 where they perished in the gas chambers.

Adele

Adele was deported from Budapest with her sister Bori to Ravensbruk, a women's concentration camp located ninety kilometers north of Berlin, to a site near the village of Ravensbruk. Ravensbruck was the site of so many horrors and hardships where 50,000 women died – either from harsh living conditions, slave labor, or execution. Prisoners were faced with forced labor and mind-numbing work moving piles of dirt from place to place. People were used as mules, harnessed to rocks as they toiled to move from one part of the camp to another.

At one point, it was decided to relocate Adele and Bori to a factory, so they found themselves on a train with other prisoners. They did not know at the time that an end to the war was imminent. When the train stopped at a station, a German officer approached them. He said the officers were going to smoke at a certain end of the platform and said, "Now is your chance to walk away". They needed no second invitation to escape. They took refuge in farms as they threaded their way home to Újfehértó.

Once they arrived, no family members greeted them. Their family had dispersed in all directions, far too many of them as ashes carried by the wind. Others had fled to other countries...anywhere but post-Nazi Hungary.

While they were there, Adele and Bori met a former family friend and neighbor, Gyula Roth. He had lost his wife and daughter to the ovens of Auschwitz and had no reason to stay. Bori decided to remain in Hungary in the meantime, but Adele had no intention of remaining. Adele said to Gyula, "You can come with me if you want, but I am not staying here."

Gyula and Adele left for a DP (displaced persons) camp in Germany where they fell in love and married. While in Germany, Adele became pregnant. The thought of a child born in Germany was too much for either of them, so they immigrated to France where they joined Gyula's brother. They stayed long enough to celebrate the birth of their first son, Robert. Two and a half years later, they all immigrated to Montréal, which became their permanent home. A year later, their second son, Asher, was born.

In 1995, the German government invited Holocaust survivors around the world to Germany to commemorate the 50th anniversary of the concentration camps.

Adele returned to Ravensbruck with her son Asher for the occasion. This time, as she walked through the gates of the former camp, she held her head high. "This is a victory for me," she said. "They wanted to kill us and I survived".

Adele's husband, Gyula, passed away in 1984. Asher talks about his parents' relationship. "I don't know how many people can say that their parents loved each other from the beginning to the end. It was not just a matter of comfort or being with someone just to alleviate loneliness. My parents were devoted to one another. Their relationship is an ideal that my brother Robert and I try to emulate in our respective lives. When my father died, it was as if Mom lost a limb. It is a loss she always remembers. Today and every day since his passing 30 years ago, she says, 'I miss your father'. Fiercely protective is a good way to describe my mom – particularly where her family is concerned. She taught me patience, strength, and most importantly, unconditional love."

"As Alzheimer's disease slowly creeps into our lives, she gave my brother and me the greatest of gifts; she gave us the chance to give her unconditional love in return. As her understanding diminishes, her feelings for her children and family remain as intense as ever and we continue to feel her love and devotion. I am so proud of my mother… she is my heroine."

Bori

Bori was deported from Budapest with her sister Adele to Ravensbruk women's concentration camp. After she was liberated, she remained in Hungary and married her husband, Pista. In 1956, they left Hungary and went to join her sister, Adele, and her brother, Mickey, in Montréal.

Erno

Erno was deported from Budapest to Mauthausen concentration camp in Austria where he endured unspeakable physical hardships, torture, and starvation. After liberation, he decided to go to Israel. First he went to Italy, and from there, boarded a boat to Palestine. As the British were limiting Jewish immigration, he was not allowed entry. Instead, he was sent to Cypress and incarcerated in a DP (displaced persons) camp. After his release in 1948, he finally reached Israel thinking that he was the sole survivor of his family.

As soon as he touched the shores of Palestine, he was immediately recruited to fight in the 1948 War of Independence where he became a demolitions expert.

His daughter Lea recalls, "After the horrors he went through at Mauthausen concentration camp, he was so happy at being given the chance to finally fight back. My father never spoke about his experiences during the war. I never even knew my father was a concentration camp survivor until I was sixteen. What I do vividly remember was how my father would scream out in fear if you touched him when waking him up in the morning. I can't even imagine the horrors he must have gone through at Mauthausen."

He first lived on Yona Hanavi Street in Tel Aviv in a one-room hovel. Then he moved to Haifa where he met his cousin Sara (Shari), also a Holocaust survivor. It was from her that he first found out that some of his siblings had survived the war. He met his future wife Sima at a movie theater. They soon fell in love and married. Their daughter Lea was born in Israel. Then they left for Montréal in 1952 and had another child, Steve.

Zoli

Zoli was deported to a forced labor camp and was never seen or heard from again.

Mickey

Mickey was deported to Auschwitz. After liberation in 1945, he returned to Újfehértó. In 1948, he moved to Montréal where he met his wife, Clara Felberman, on a blind date that was set up by Clara's aunts. They fell in love and were married March 4, 1951. They had two daughters, Margaret and Shirli.

Sanyi

Sanyi was taken to a forced labor camp and then was sent to Siberia where he was put in a prisoner of war camp with captured German soldiers. In one conversation my mother had with him a year before he passed away in 1996, she recalls him mentioning that he once found German soldiers eating meat in the camp. He was surprised because food was so scarce and none of the prisoners received meat. When he asked the German soldiers where they had gotten meat from, they told Sanyi that they had cooked some of the flesh from someone who had frozen to death the day before. Some of the accounts are so horrific, they are almost impossible to believe. Unfortunately, they are true and paint a grotesque portrait of humanity. After the war, Sanyi returned to Hungary and married Zsuzsi. They left Hungary in 1956 and went to live in New York. They had one son named Ronnie.

Olga

Olga was deported to Auschwitz, Kaufering, and Bergen-Belsen concentration camps. She was liberated from Bergen-Belsen in 1945. She was taken to Sweden for medical treatment and then left for the United States in 1947.

Eva

Eva was deported to Auschwitz, Kaufering, and Bergen-Belsen concentration camps together with my mother. She died three weeks after liberation from Bergen-Belsen in 1945.

The Roth family at Stanley's (Asher's)
Bar Mitzvah celebration. (l-r): Robert,
Adele, Stanley (Asher), Gyula, 1964.

Bori and her husband Pista, 1964.

Erno as a soldier in the War of
Independence, 1948, Israel.

Erno and his wife Sima, 1964.

Sanyi and Zsuzsi, and their son Ronny, 1973.

Wedding of Mickey and Clara, Montréal, 1951.

Reaching the New World

Bella and my mother arrived in New York Harbor on January 27, 1947.

"When we disembarked from the ship, Uncle Harry, Aunt Minnie, Uncle Adolf, Aunt Margaret, and Aunt Pauline were there to greet us. From New York Harbor, we first went to Aunt Margaret's house where we finally met our cousins, Ida and Dorothy."

"Bella and I moved in with Aunt Pauline in Newark, New Jersey for the first few months. Then we stayed at Aunt Margaret's house, also in Newark. Bella and I soon found work in the garment industry in ladies suits and coats. Bella worked in Newark and I traveled ninety minutes to New York City."

While living in Newark, my mother became good friends with Helen Kaufman.

LAST KNOWN SURVIVORS of
Jewish family of 14 in Budapest, si-
ters Bella Newman (left), 30, and
Olga Colt, New World arrivals, ar-
awed by view of city from the H.rd-
ion, off 57th St. Nazis killed parents
and two other sisters. Rest of family
is missing, presumed dead.

Bella and my mother gaze in awe from the boat
as they reach New York Harbor.[75]

---

[75] Reprinted with the express permission of the New Jersey Mirror, courtesy of the Burlington County Times.

(l-r): Helen Kaufman stands with my mother,
Olga Czik, summer, 1949.

The first meeting with cousins Ida and Dorothy
(daughters of Aunt Margaret and Uncle Adolf).
(l-r) Sitting on the couch: Dorothy, my mother, Bella, Ida.
(l-r) Standing: Uncle Adolf, Aunt Margaret.

Helen Kaufman

Helen Kaufman was a Holocaust survivor born on December 17, 1925 in Beregovo, Czechoslovakia. She was one of three brothers, three sisters and one half-brother.[76]

In 1944, Helen and her family were taken to the Beregszasz ghetto where they stayed for several weeks before being deported to Auschwitz. At Auschwitz, she was separated from her family and given a number which was tattooed across her arm. Helen endured cruel beatings, starvation and hard labor. Several months later, Helen was deported to Bergen-Belsen, where she became very ill.

After finally being liberated by the British, Helen was sent to Göteborg (also known as Gothenburg), Sweden to receive medical treatment for the illnesses she had contracted during her time in the concentration camps.

After Helen recovered, she found work in a cotton factory. While in Sweden, Helen's paternal Aunt Rose from Newark saw an ad Helen had put in the newspaper seeking relatives. She immediately contacted Helen, arranged the immigration documents, and sent her a ticket.

After losing almost all of her family in Auschwitz, Helen arrived in New York Harbor in January 1948. She moved in with her Aunt Rose in Newark where she met Olga Czik. They became good friends and often double-dated together.

---

[76] Lipiner, Michael. Magyar, Stars & Stripes: a Journey From Hungary Through the Holocaust and to New York. New York: iUniverse, 2005

The Love Apartment

In September 1948, Bella and my mother moved to the Bronx and rented a room in "Fischer Nanny's" (Nanny is pronounced "nay nee") apartment. "Nanny" literally means "aunt" in Hungarian but is a title of respect for older women.

In March, 1949, Bella met her husband, Menyus. They married and lived in Queens. Bella and my mother always remained extremely close until Bella passed away in 1980.

My mother recalls, "After I met George and got engaged, Helen decided to move in with me and soon she too met the love of her life. After Helen got married, Menyus's cousin, Eta, who was already in her late twenty's, decided that anyone who moved in with Fischer Nanny would surely marry. Shortly after Eta moved in with her, she too found a husband."

Bella and her husband, Menyus, in front of their
apartment house in Queens, 1970.

Chapter 4

My Parents Marry

My Father and Mother Meet

Alex Taub lived near the *Hotel Marseilles* on 103rd Street, just two blocks away from Laci's house, where many Hungarian immigrants from that area, including Alex and my father, used to hang around. When asked how he and my father met, Alex said, "George used to stop and listen to what we [the other Hungarian immigrants] were talking about. Eventually George and I became good friends."

Saturday nights they would often go together to the *Kossuth Ballroom* at a hotel in downtown Manhattan, a place frequented by many young, single Hungarian refugees.[77]

It was there, in October, 1949, that my father met my mother, Olga Czik. After two months of dating, my father fell in love with her and asked for her hand in marriage.

My mother and father after their engagement.

[77] Lipiner, Michael. Magyar, Stars & Stripes: a Journey from Hungary Through the Holocaust and to New York. New York: iUniverse, 2005.

The Wedding

My parents married at Ancsi and Laci's house on February 19, 1950. My father's sister Aranka and her family were still in Sweden at the time. Since they were unable to attend, they sent a telegram to my parents one day before the wedding with their heart filled wishes.

Although my mother's parents were no longer alive, all of her father's siblings attended her wedding, including her sister Bella and her brother Mickey who had just arrived from Europe the year before. Her good friend, Helen Kaufman, from New Jersey also attended.

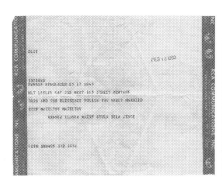

The telegram sent by Aranka to my father and his new bride.

(l-r): My parents, Mickey (my mother's brother), Bella (my mother's sister), and her husband, Menyus.

My mother signs the Ketubah[78] while my father stands next to her smiling with happiness. His good friend, Alex Taub, (stands in back of my mother), also attended their wedding.

Alex Taub was also one of the two witnesses that signed the Ketubah.

---

[78] A Jewish marriage contract.

My father performed the Veiling Ceremony (bedeken). During the bedeken, the groom covers the bride's face with the veil and recites the blessing Rebecca received from her mother and brother before she left to marry Isaac (*Genesis 24:60*).

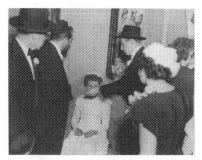

My father covers his bride's face.

Flanked by his brother, Laci, and his wife, Ancsi, my father watches as his bride makes her way to the chuppah (the bridal canopy).

My parents, under the chuppah where the marriage ceremony takes place. At the end, the groom traditionally breaks a glass, which symbolizes the destruction of the ancient Temple in Jerusalem in the first century.

(l-r): Laci, my parents, Ancsi
Stanley (l), Kenny (r).

The happy couple!

All of my maternal grandfather's siblings and their families
attended the wedding, taken in Laci's living room.

My parents' wedding turned out to be a lucky day also for Alex Taub and Helen Kaufman. At the wedding (which happened to fall on Alex's birthday), Alex was introduced to Helen and they immediately fell in love!

Helen and Alex were married just a few months later, on June 18, 1950, at the *Congregation Machziki Horan* Synagogue in the Bronx. My mother and father were invited to the wedding where my father was Alex's best man.

My Mother's Personal Victory Against Hitler

After my parents married, they remained at Laci's house living in a one-room apartment, where they shared a bathroom with Aranka, and her husband, Gyula. My father found a new job at the Lewyt vacuum cleaner factory. My mother continued to work until she gave birth to my sister, Evelyn, on June 28, 1952.

When she gave birth, her first thought was this was her victory over Hitler. Hitler had set out to exterminate all Jews through his plan "The Final Solution" - his plan to annihilate the Jewish people. But she, with her first child, knew she had won. This was her personal victory against Hitler. Hitler had failed. She had defeated him.

In 1952, my parents became naturalized American citizens and legally changed their name from Klein to Kay. They lived in Laci's apartment house on 105th Street in Manhattan until I was born on February 13, 1956.

My parents, my sister, and me in front of Laci's office, 1956.

Spending Time in Pleasantville

Grateful that they were able to escape Nazi Europe, Laci and Ancsi wanted their children, Kenny and Stanley, to enjoy the tranquility and freedom in the United States that they did not have in Europe. In 1949, they bought a small house in Pleasantville, a village in Westchester County, New York, where they spent their weekends and summers.

In Pleasantville, Kenny and Stanley grew up experiencing the peace and serenity of nature, roaming freely in the forests, swimming in nearby Bear Ridge Lake, riding their bicycles, and playing softball in the streets.

Laci would invite his extended family as well as friends to join them in Pleasantville. In 1950, after they were married, my parents joined Laci and Ancsi on their trips.

In 1952, when my mother was pregnant with my sister, Evelyn, just seven years after being liberated from Bergen-Belsen, my parents bought a small, one-bedroom house just up the street from Laci and Ancsi in Pleasantville. My sister and I would eventually spend many memorable years there. Once my parents bought the house, they also invited my mother's extended family to spend time with them there. In 1964, Erno's children, Lea and Steve, spent a nostalgic summer in Pleasantville together with us. My Aunt Bella and her husband, Menyus, also became frequent visitors in Pleasantville.

Bella was like the grandmother we never had. We all loved her dearly and she loved us dearly in return. We were devastated when she passed away in 1980. After Bella died, Adele's son, Stanley Roth, commemorated her death by officially changing his name to Asher, in honor of Bella's son, Asher, who died in the gas chambers at Auschwitz.

An inseparable part of the Pleasantville experience was Laci's dog, Lady. Lady was gentle, lovable, and good-natured. She was a "lady" in every sense of the word, and our constant companion. As the "older" cousin, my cousin Stanley took an active role in teaching both my sister and me how to ride bicycles and swim.

Laci and Ancsi hosted not only friends and family from America, but also family from overseas. In 1953, my Aunt Bözsi's son, Simcha (Simmi), from Israel, spent some time with the family in Pleasantville. We also had fun in the winters when Bear Ridge Lake would freeze over. The cousins would join us ice skating on the frozen lake. How fortunate my parents, and all their siblings felt that they were able to bring up their children in peace and harmony. How fortunate they felt for even being alive.

My mother is pregnant with my sister, Evelyn in front of our house in Pleasantville, 1952.

Bella, stands with my sister, Evelyn (left), and me (right), in front of Laci's house in Pleasantville, 1960.

Back, (l-r): Judy, Lea, Evelyn
Front: Steve, 1964.

My sister and I stand in front of
Laci's house with Lady, 1960.

Back, (l-r): Menyus (Bella's husband),
Aranka (holding Evelyn), Laci. Front (l-r):
Mary, Simmi Bretter (Bözsi's son), 1953.

Stanley teaches me to bike ride, April, 1963.

Moving On

In 1956, my parents moved to another apartment in Woodside, Queens, where they only stayed for a year. Then we moved to a one-bedroom apartment on the fifth floor of 664 W. 163rd St. in Manhattan, and then, around the corner to a two-bedroom apartment on 97 Fort Washington Ave.

In 1964, my parents made two important decisions. After the Lewyt vacuum cleaner factory went out of business, my father decided to buy his own taxi medallion, and in 1965, they sold their house in Pleasantville and bought a house in Flushing, Queens.

The Kay house on 150-66 Booth Memorial Ave. in Flushing, Queens.

My father's taxi parked in back of our house in Flushing.

My Parents Revisit Hungary

My parents returned to Hungary in 1971. My father had no desire to step foot in Hungary again, but he did want to visit his mother's grave. Three years later in 1974, Laci brought my grandmother's remains to Segula Cemetery in Petach Tikva, Israel, together with other members of the family who passed away before the Holocaust.

During their trip, they went to see my father's former house in Szécsény. In Salgótarján, they went to visit Mr. Löwinger, the man with whom my father had studied to be a dental mechanic. Mr. Löwinger had been married before the war but lost his wife in the Holocaust. In Nagybátony, they visited my father's cousin, Adolf Weiss, whose wife Rózsi had perished in the war.

In 1979, my mother returned with her sister Bella to visit their home town Újfehértó. "It did not develop at all since we had left. When I was living there, it was so beautiful. Now, it looks so run down. When we got there, we went to visit some of our former neighbors. Some of them were willing to meet us, but others were not."

"One of my neighbors, Manyi, was very happy to see us, but her husband refused to talk to us. In 1944 after we were deported, Manyi and her husband moved in and took over our house. When Bori, Adele, and Mickey came back to Újfehértó after the war, they demanded the house back. Manyi's husband gave them a hard time. He didn't want to leave. My sisters and brother offered to sell them the house, but they did not want to buy it. Eventually they managed to evict them but he was still angry for being forced to leave our house."

My parents, in front of my father's house in Szécsény, 1971.

Our Trip to Hungary – Personal Reflections

In the summer of 2001, my mother, my sister, and I took a trip to Hungary where we visited both my parents' houses in Szécsény and Újfehértó. Evelyn describes what it was like for her to be in the places that had been part of our parents' past.

"All my life, I had been lucky enough to hear about where I came from, my heritage, all my traditions. I heard many stories, mostly from my mother, and I eagerly listened."

"As I remembered hearing descriptions about what their homes looked like, I tried to picture their way of life in my mind - their town, their house, my mother's garden, the railroad tracks next to my father's family restaurant. There were images of horses and buggies, trains, different kinds of fruit trees, the well in my mother's backyard. But they were all just images."

"Then, in June, 2001, my mother put together a very exciting trip; a heritage trip I would call it. She took me and my sister, Judy, to Hungary to get a first hand view of some of the things they had told me. My father had already been to Hungary with my mother and did not want to go back again so it was just the three of us. I joined up with my mother and Judy in Hungary as I was flying from New York and they were leaving from Israel."

"We drove from Budapest with a local guide, to Szécsény, to my father's home. Arriving there, it was exactly as I had pictured it; but at the same time it was all so new to me. It was all there - the restaurant that was connected to their small house, and the train station that was right next to it. The roads were dirt roads and they were dusty and there weren't many people around. The restaurant was in disarray, as the owner of the house was dismantling it. The home was well kept and up to date inside. How did I know? The owner of the house happened to be there and allowed us to look around. We took pictures of everything and posed in the same place as my dad and his family once posed many years ago. We have that beautiful picture of them. That picture connected me to everything I had been told about what his home town looked like. It was very special. I told my father after we had returned that I thought his house was a "big" house, as compared to Mommy's, but he said it was small. I guess that's how he remembered it. But then, he was a young man when he left and that's what he remembered. I just wish he had told us more."

"From there we went to my mother's home town of Újfehértó. This time, we had a personal guide, my mother, to take us through and describe everything. She tried very hard to remember how she went from her home to her school, to the stores, and from place to place. The cherry tree she spoke so much about and the well they had at the side of their house, were both there, just as she had told me so many times. This is the same well her neighbors used to come to for Tashlich[79]. It was so special to her as this was all part of her life and childhood. It was not supposed to be taken from her, torn apart from her, but it was. Her memories are something that couldn't be ripped from my mother. Again, at this part of the trip, we were lucky enough to be able to look into the house that she once called her home. I was eager to walk in, to see the rooms that once housed my grandparents and their ten children. I stuck my head in and was so surprised to find a kitchen, a "living room", and another room. I had expected more than that. How did they all fit? I was stumped. It's amazing how much we take for granted today, "needing" enough space, while my parents were so happy just being with their family in whatever space they had. My mother took us through the town, at times finding it difficult to remember just exactly where everything was, but she did a good job. We also went to see the monument there that was erected listing the names of all the Jews murdered during the Holocaust."

"Going on this trip was so special to me. The look on my mother's face was enough to light up the sky, at times, and at other times I saw

---

[79] The word "Tashlich" means to cast off in Hebrew. It is a ritual that is observed on the first day of Rosh Hashana (the Jewish New Year), which involves symbolically casting the sins of the previous year by tossing pieces of bread into a body of water.

the sadness as she remembered the good times of her childhood and her family, especially the people she never got to see again. For me, it was like going back in time. Once we entered these towns, it felt like we were leaving behind all the modern conveniences. I observed people still using their horses to get around on the unpaved roads that wrapped themselves around the small buildings, homes and stores. There were all the expected things, like telephones, electricity, cars, and so on, but the feeling of the "olden days" permeated deep into me. My family and my traditions always meant so much to me and having had the chance to really be a part of it truly solidified it. My parents' stories and experiences meant so much more to me after this trip. They say that a picture tells a thousand words. Well, that is certainly an understatement."

"I remember talking about my trip with my father some time later. I remember the smile on his face and how his eyes lit up when we told him about all the things we saw, every little detail. I told him that the descriptions he had given us of his town before we left helped so much as we walked around. It was almost like having him with us on the trip."

"This is an experience I'll never forget and I can't thank them enough for giving me the opportunity to be a part of their whole lives. I hope that one, day my children and grandchildren will have the same opportunity to visit these places, so that they can pass down to their children the excitement they can feel knowing where we came from."

My mother, my sister Evelyn, and I, stand in front
of my father's house in Szécsény, 2001.

My mother stands in front of her house in Újfehértó, 2001.

Next to the monument, my mother points to the name of the Bella's son, (György) Asher Neumann.

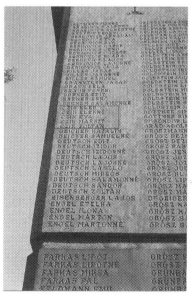

At the top: The names of the family members of my mother's uncle, Lajos Berkovics: Berkovics Lajos Lajosné (Lajos and his wife Sara), their three children, Olga, Eva, and Joseph. Further down: The names of Czik Elek and Czik Elekne (my mother's parents), and her three siblings who perished: Eva, Margaret (Margit), and Zoltan (Zoli).

Returning to the Land
of Our Forefathers

As a young girl, there were so many things I did not know about my father. He spoke very little about his past. Later on in life, when my sister and I would ask him about his life in Hungary, his parents, his relatives, his memories, he would open up somewhat. Looking back, I regret not finding out more about my grandparents while I still could have. After reading his poetry in which he describes how much he missed his family, I felt that talking about them might have been too painful for him. I also did not know about his feelings for Israel or that he spoke fluent Hebrew.

Despite the fact that he decided to leave Palestine, his passion and love for Eretz Yisrael never dwindled. He knew that one day he would return to the Jewish homeland.

I remember on May 15, 1974, I came home one evening and found my father with tears streaming down his face. He was watching the gruesome news on television about a terrorist attack in Ma'alot, Israel, in which Arab terrorists had massacred twenty-two Israeli high school students. He was beyond grief. After that, my father set the process of returning to Israel in motion.

At that point, I had started my first semester of college at Queens College. My father asked me if I would consider going to Israel for one year on an overseas student program. I immediately agreed. In November, 1974, I left America to spend the next year studying at Tel Aviv University. After just a few months in Israel, I understood that Israel was the home of the Jews and I was there to stay.

One year later, Laci and Ancsi decided to move to Israel, partially at the behest of Rebbe (Rabbi in Yiddish) Yekusiel Yehudah Halberstam, the founder of the famous Sanz Rabbinic Dynasty. Rebbe Halberstam was a Holocaust survivor who had lost 150 members of his immediate and extended family, including his wife and eleven children. After being shot during the war, he made a vow to G-d that if he recovered and survived the war, he would build a hospital in Israel. He survived the war and rebuilt his life when he married his second wife and had seven more children. They moved to the United States for a few years where the Rebbe became a patient of Dr. Leslie Kay (Laci). In addition to the doctor/patient relationship, they developed a great deal of respect for one another.

In 1960, the Rebbe decided to fulfill the vow he made with G-d. He moved back to Israel permanently and spent fifteen years raising the funds needed to establish Laniado Hospital, in Kiryat Sanz, Netanya.

In 1974, on one of the Rebbe's trips to New York, he visited Laci and told him of his plans for a new hospital in Netanya. Recognizing Dr. Kay as a talented and devoted physician, the Rebbe asked him to join the Laniado staff and help establish the obstetrics department. Laci happily accepted. In 1975, Laci and Ancsi moved to Israel and Laci began to work in Laniado Hospital. He was not only instrumental in establishing the obstetrics department, but also helped to develop and expand the nascent hospital's other departments and services. Rebbe Halberstam remained a devoted patient of Laci's, refusing to be treated by any other doctor.

Laci and Ancsi bought an apartment in Netanya along the picturesque seaside. Their balcony overlooked the beach and together they used to love watching the sun set over the water.

In 1985, after my father retired, my parents moved to Israel. They bought an apartment in Netanya, just one block away from Laci and Ancsi. My parents, and Laci and Ancsi, spent many happy days together on the beautiful Netanya beach and were just glad to be close to one another again. Aranka moved to Israel in 1990.

Although my mother found herself having to adjust to living in a country whose language she did not speak, she adapted remarkably well. There were a large number of English and Hungarian speaking people in Netanya, and in addition, she found that most Israelis were able to speak conversational English. Despite the language barrier, with my mother's inherent goodness, her desire to help everyone, and her natural kindness, she always managed to capture everyone's heart, no matter what language they spoke.

By the time my parents made Aliyah to Israel, I was already married and had two children. We were living in Tel Aviv at the time and my parents often came to visit my children, Ayelet and Ori. If I needed a babysitter on a workday, my parents would leave Netanya at 5:00am in order to get to my house before I had to leave for work. My parents and I spent many summers at my sister's house in New York where my children, and hers, would cherish the time they spent with each other.

In 2008, my father was diagnosed with Parkinson's disease. As my father's limbs became stiffer and stiffer it became more difficult for him to walk. When my father's health began to decline my mother's role changed from one of loving wife to dedicated nurse. She was always at his side and always put him before herself. As he started to fall more often, my mother felt that she could no longer take care of him by herself so they hired a caregiver to take care of my father twenty-four hours a day.

My Father's Love for Chess

My father learned how to play, and love, the game of chess in Hungary. He continued to play while he was living in Palestine and then passed on his love for the game on to his grandchildren, great-grandchildren, and others. He always showed great patience with every game and took pleasure in instructing his opponents in the best strategy.

In 1988, I moved to Sha'arei Tikva and my parents spent much time with us. A neighbor of mine, Tomer Heller, an especially kind and gentle young man, would come to play chess with my father. Although they were two generations apart, they immediately bonded. Despite my father's advanced age, he remained an avid and skilled chess player. Sometimes when I would walk into the dining room where they were playing, I would see them just talking, almost like old friends. My father enjoyed Tomer's visits immensely.

Tomer reminisces, "I vividly remember the opportunities I had to go and play chess with George when he spent time with his family in Sha'arei Tikva. It is a game I enjoy very much, largely due to George, but I now seldom play. Alongside the game, he would tell me stories about his personal history and life story, and we would discuss general history. He gave me a chance to sharpen my English as well as my chess! George was a special person and made many of my days with him very enjoyable. I will remember him fondly."

My father spent many hours playing chess with my grandson, Itai, who not only learned to love the game and become a skilled chess player, but even more, he learned to cherish the many hours he spent playing chess with his great-grandfather, "Papa".

Playing chess with his great-grandson Itai, Ayelet's son.

Noa, Ayelet's daughter, sits with Itai during one
of his many chess games with Papa.

Playing chess with his grandson Ronen, Evelyn's son, 2004.

Playing chess with his grandson Dovev, Evelyn's son, 2001.

Playing chess with his newfound friend, Tomer, 2013.

My Father, the Family Man

My father was a very spiritual man. He never had any need for material possessions. The two things he valued most were his devotion to his family and extended family, and Eretz Yisrael. Nothing else was important for him.

He and my mother were always surrounded by family and present for all family occasions. They remained close with all their grandchildren: Evelyn's children Dovev, Ronen, and Yael in America, and my children, Ayelet and Ori in Israel.

My parents at Dovev's Bar Mitzvah, 1989

(l-r): My mother, Ronen and his wife Simmie,
Evelyn's husband, Moshe, my father, 2002.

My parents and I at my daughter, Ayelet's wedding, 2004.

My father together with my son, Ori, at Ayelet's wedding, 2004.

My father gets emotional at his youngest grandchild,
Yael's (Evelyn's daughter) wedding, 2006.

Last Family Photos with My Father

As my father's health slowly began to deteriorate, both Ronen and Dovev traveled to Israel with their families in 2013 for what was to be the last time they were to see their grandfather.

Yael, her husband Dovi with my parents.

Front, (l-r): Simmie (Ronen's wife) with Maya (Ronen and Simmie's daughter), my father, Itai.
Next row, (l-r): Evelyn with Eliana (Ronen and Simmie's daughter), Ronen stands in back of Evelyn, Judy, Ayelet's daughter Noa stands in back of my father, my mother, Roi (Ayelet's husband), and Ayelet stands in front of Roi, holding her daughter Maya.

My sister and I with our father, our last photo together, 2013.

(l-r): Dovev's wife, Shayna, with their son Moshe Tzvi on her lap, me, their daughter Nili, my parents, their daughter Rena, Dovev.

Chapter 5

My Father's Legacy

The Value of Silence

My father's last five years with Parkinson's disease were not easy for him. Three years before his death, he fell and paralyzed his right arm. A year later, he broke his hip, and was wheelchair-bound till his death. He was trapped inside his body, but he never complained. Only once, when I went to visit my parents and asked my father how he was feeling, he said to me with profound sadness, "Judy, I am in a wheelchair". I felt heartbroken because there was nothing I could do to help him.

The only part of his body he was able to move, albeit with great difficulty, was his left hand. He used his left hand to continue playing chess until his last day. One of the most heartbreaking moments occurred while I was watching my father and Itai play chess. He picked up a bishop and sadly said, "Judy, I can't remember the name of this chess piece. Please remind me what it is called".

My father was a man of few words. He was extremely quiet, and never said anything redundant. Whenever he did speak, he chose his words carefully. He avoided speaking badly about others, an important Jewish value. He was always honest, without exception. He was a modest, simple man, never needing anything of glitter.

My father's silent ways had a profound effect on all his children and grandchildren. During his lifetime, he was always humble and respectful. He taught us the value of silence. The Torah teaches us that a quiet sound can sometimes be the most powerful force. In his silence, he taught us humility and modesty. He left us in silence, in his own very powerful way, leaving his mark.

One of the most serious sins in Judaism is the sin of *lashon hara* (literally meaning "evil tongue"), saying negative things about a person or discrediting a person in any way. In Psalm 34:14, it says, "Guard your tongue from evil and your lips from speaking deceit". My father never violated this prohibition; he observed it to the fullest.

After my father passed away, the rabbi of my town, Rabbi Shmuel Feuerstein, came to visit us while we were sitting *shiva*[80]. He asked me what characterized my father the most. I told him that he knew how to guard his tongue and never slandered anyone in any way. Rabbi Feuerstein asked me how old my father was when he passed away. When I told him he died just two days before his 94th birthday, he smiled as if something just became very clear to him. He said that the Hafetz Haim[81], who wrote a book on Jewish ethics regarding the laws of speech, was rewarded with longevity for observing the Jewish laws of *lashon hara*. The Hafetz Haim was 94 years old when he died. My father was also blessed with a long life. He was 94 when he passed away, just like the Hafetz Haim.

My parents in my home in Sha'arei Tikva, 2013.

---

[80] Shiva is a seven-day period of intense mourning that follows burial. The observance of shiva applies to a person who has lost a parent, spouse, sibling, or child.

[81] Rabbi Israel Meir HaCohen Kagan, commonly known as the "Chafetz Haim," was born in Zhetel, Poland on February 6, 1838. He wrote several books on the importance of guarding one's tongue.

The Almighty's Guiding Hand

My father is greatly missed. Everyone remembers him as a modest and gentle soul. My father passed away in my home on a Sunday morning. In Judaism, the concept of Divine Providence teaches us that G-d determines every event in our lives and nothing in this world happens by chance. My father was not supposed to be at my house. My mother had been hospitalized the Thursday afternoon before due to high blood pressure, and spent the weekend in the hospital. So I brought my father to spend *Shabbat* with me in my house. Looking back, I am happy that my mother did not have to witness his passing. In this, I clearly see the guiding hand of G-d.

My grandson Itai had a very special bond with my father. Itai and my father often played chess together and he would constantly be hugging my father. One of the most touching moments I remember was when my father was in a rehabilitation home after he broke his hip. My daughter, Ayelet, came with her two children, Itai and Noa, to visit my father. Seeing that my father was almost completely incapacitated and unable to feed himself, Itai (at five years old), picked up the yogurt sitting on my father's dinner tray and started to feed him. The compassion he felt for his great-grandfather brought tears to my eyes.

On Saturday night, the evening before he died, Itai walked into the kitchen where my father was, went over to him, and gave him such a big kiss and hug that my father smiled from ear to ear. My father looked at him and said "What a sweet child". Looking back, I see this as Itai's farewell kiss to my father, little did he know.

The next morning, I found my father unconscious, bleeding profusely from his mouth and nose. I called the ambulance and the medics tried for an hour and a half to revive him, but to no avail. He died peacefully and in no pain. He never regained consciousness.

Words that flow from an innocent child's mouth are always words of truth. Later that day, Itai came to me, and said, "Grandma, do you know where we should bury Papa? In the Machpelah cave[82]". For Itai, my father belonged among the ranks of our righteous forefathers of the Bible, Abraham, Isaac, and Jacob.

I do believe that Itai's soul knew when my father's last day was going to be and that G-d arranged for them to be together so they could see each other for the last time. My father died on Itai's birthday, testimony to the special bond the two of them had.

Finally, Yonatan Michael, Ayelet's fourth child, was born on February 2, 2015, and bears my father's Hebrew name, Michael.

---

[82] The Machpelah cave is the cave in Hebron, which was purchased by the patriarch Abraham for the purpose of burying his wife Sarah after she died. It is one of the holiest places in *Eretz Yisrael*. Later on, Abraham was also buried there. Subsequently, it became the final resting place for all the patriarchs and matriarchs (with the exception of Rachel, who died in childbirth on the way to Bethlehem).

Itai, giving his great-grandfather a farewell kiss.

Itai with his beloved great-grandfather.

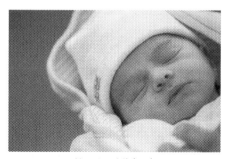

Yonatan Michael

Epilogue

NAMES, NOT NUMBERS

As the generation of the Holocaust survivors are slowly dying off, and the number of Holocaust deniers are growing, a group of twenty-one eighth grade students from Yeshiva Har Torah in New York participated in a program where they interviewed Holocaust survivors.

The name of the program, started in 2011, is called ***Names, Not Numbers***. These interviews not only bear testimony against deniers of the Holocaust and keep the memories of the Holocaust alive, but also continue to educate the world about this horrific time period.

As the last generation to come in contact with Holocaust survivors and listen to their stories, they wanted to relay the messages to future generations and the rest of the world.

Yael Greenberger, Evelyn's daughter, who works in Yeshiva Har Torah, had wanted her grandmother to participate in this program when the program first started, but my mother would not travel overseas while my father's health was deteriorating.

After my father passed away, my mother traveled to New York to visit my sister in 2014. While she was there, she was invited to take part in the program.

From the earliest possible moment in our lives, my mother decided that she must tell her story to her children so that the memories of the Holocaust could be passed on and never forgotten.

The young students that had the privilege of taking part in this program were touched not only by my mother's courage, but also her struggle to ensure that memories of the Holocaust would never die out.

My mother was in turn inspired by the determination of these students to be part of the effort to keep Holocaust memories alive.

"I am so happy to be here and to have participated in this wonderful program. To everyone who participated in this program, you should know how very important it is. You are passing down to your generation, and future generations, what went on during World War II and how it affected millions of people. It is your responsibility to carry on the memories of our mothers, fathers, children, sisters and brothers who are not here to tell their stories. I am very lucky to be here and see the beautiful faces of our descendants; you who are sitting here, learning in Yeshivas, and keeping our traditions. You have the good fortune to carry on our legacy and to tell the world that we were not defeated and to make sure it never happens again."

"The importance of this evening ensures our future generations that we will not be forgotten. Thank you, Yael, for telling me about this. I am so proud to be part of this, but most of all, I am so proud to be your Grandma."

True to her word, my mother continues to encourage her children, grandchildren, and even her great-grandchildren to remain part of the effort to keep the Holocaust memories alive. On April 15, 2015, she attended Holocaust Remembrance Day in Sha'arei Tikva, Israel, with me, and my six-year-old granddaughter, Noa.

My mother receives an invitation to participate in the Holocaust
film project produced by Yeshiva Har Torah's eight grade students.

May 15, 2014
ט״ו אייר תשע״ד

Dear Mrs. Kay,

We would like to thank you for your contribution to the Names, Not Numbers program.

Your story really touched not only our hearts, but the hearts of everyone with whom your story will be shared.

We remember an account you shared with us during your interview that had a strong impact on us. You explained to us that you had been giving food to a German family and had missed your curfew. You were walking back to your barracks when you saw your friends motioning that you should run. You turned around and saw that an S.S soldier was holding a rifle gun and was about to shoot you. As you started to run, he shot multiple times, but missed. It is a true miracle that you survived that event without being harmed.

This left an impression on us because it taught us that even in the darkest times Hashem is still watching over us.

We really appreciate the amazing contribution you made to our project. Your story will continue to live on and help fight against deniers of the Holocaust.

Thank you for being an inspiration to all of us.

Sincerely,

Shira Friedman, Jordy Gross, Hannah Shulman, and Bruriah Sloan

A letter of thanks my mother received from
the students at Yeshiva Har Torah.

In this photograph, my mother stands with the students who interviewed her. (l-r): Shira Friedman, Hannah Schulman, Ms. Sarah Manasseh, my mother, Yael, Jordana Gross, Bruriah Sloan.

(l-r): Me, Noa my granddaughter (Ayelet's daughter), my mother.

In Memory of our Dear Husband, Father, Grandfather, and Great-grandfather

After I wrote this poem, I read it to Itai, and told him that I wrote it for Papa. I mentioned though, that I did not have a title for the poem. Itai said to me, "Grandma, let's name it, *The Eyes and Heart of Love.*"

The Eyes and Heart of Love

By Judy Cohen

Gaze into your eyes and reach your heart
Your silence reaches the inner depths of your soul
Reverberating from within
Where your cloaked passions
Lay restlessly imprisoned amidst the shadows of the dark abyss

Close your eyes and see the sun
Turn away and touch the sky
Wrap the tears inside your golden song
And you need no longer weep

You followed your last path
And blended into the tapestry
Hidden inside the complete work
You made it glow even brighter

And the tide rushes in to wash away another glittering grain of sand

Printed in the United States
By Bookmasters